2nd edition

NEW YORK'S
100 BEST

Little Places to Shop

Eve Claxton

Illustrations by
Claudia Pearson

A CITY & COMPANY GUIDE • NEW YORK

Dedication

To my mum, who can be just as happy at ABC Carpet & Home as
she is at The Met, and my dad, who wouldn't want to go to one
store, let alone 100.

Acknowledgements
Thanks to Helene, Melisa, and everyone at City & Company; Claudia
Pearson for the collaboration, and Heather Zschock for designing.
Special thanks to Brandon; Hannah MacDonald for advising and
Hannah Weaver for teaching me the power of retail therapy. Big
thanks to my sisters Ruth and Hannah for being beautiful.

Publisher's Note:
Neither City & Company nor the author has any interest, financial or
personal, in the locations listed in this book. No fees were paid or services rendered in exchange for inclusion in these pages. Hours vary
from store to store and season to season, and stores can close down or
change hands at a moment's notice. It's advisable to call ahead before
making a special visit. All area codes are 212 unless otherwise noted.

About the Author

Eve Claxton writes for *Time Out New York* magazine and other publications. She was born in London and lives, writes, and shops in New York City. She is the author of *New York's 50 Best Bookstores for Book Lovers*, also published by City & Company.

About the llustrator

Claudia Pearson illustrates for a wide variety of clients including *The New York Times* and Neiman Marcus. She was born in London, currently lives in Brooklyn, and runs her own store, Tink, in Manhattan.

CONTENTS

Stores by Neighborhood 4
Stores by Category 6
Introduction 12
Appendices 150
   Best for Discounts 150
   The Department Stores 151
   The Best of the Flagships 153
Alphabetical Index 156

Stores by neighborhood

UPPER EAST SIDE

Betsey Bunky Nini 15
Big City Kite Co. 16
Billy Martin's 17
Cambridge Chemists 18
Dollhouse Antics 19
En Soie 20
Kitchen Arts & Letters 22
MacKenzie-Childs 23
Out of the Closet 25
Shanghai Tang 26
Tender Buttons 27
Time Will Tell 29

UPPER WEST SIDE
AND HARLEM

Upper West Side

Allan & Suzi 32
The Ballet Company 33
Bath Island 34
Hudson Dry Goods 35
Maxilla & Mandible 36
Olive & Bette's 37
Only Hearts 39

Harlem

Mona Hair Center 40

MIDTOWN

Alberene Cashmeres 43
Art of Shaving 44
As Seen on TV 45
B&H Photo-Video
   and Pro Audio 46
The Complete Traveller 47
Doggie-Do and
   Pussycats, Too! 48
Eve's Garden 48
Felissimo 50
Fifth Avenue
   Chocolatière 52

La Crasia a.k.a.
Glove Street 53
Manny's Millinery 54
Manny's Music 55
Nat Sherman 56
Nicolina 57
Soho Woman on the
Park 59
SSS Nice Price 60
Takashimaya 61

CHELSEA AND THE FLATIRON DISTRICT

Chelsea

Candleschtick 64
Dave's 65
Jazz Record Center 66
Jeffrey NY 67

Flatiron District

ABC Carpet & Home 69
Academy Records and CDs . .70
The Fan Club 71
Fishs Eddy 72
Just Bulbs 73
Paragon Sporting Goods 74
Reminiscence 75

WEST VILLAGE

Alphaville 78
Aphrodisia 79
Bigelow Chemist 80
Bombalulu's 81
Chelsea Garden Center Home . .82
Hudson Street Papers 83
Jerry Ohlinger's Movie
Material Store 84
Mxyplyzyk 85
Three Lives & Co. 86
Village Chess Shop 88

EAST VILLAGE AND LOWER EAST SIDE

Alphabets 90
Anna .91
Bond 07 92
Footlight Records 94
H 95
Kiehl's 96
Other Music 98

Quilted Corner 99
Resurrection 100
Savoia 102
Strand Bookstore 103
Sol Moscot Opticians 104
TG-170 106
Timtoum 107
Tink .108

SOHO

Broadway Panhandler 111
Enchanted Forest 112
Fragments 113
Grass Roots Garden 115
The Hat Shop 116
Hotel Venus 118
Kate's Paperie 119
Le Corset 121
Otto Tootsi Plohound 123
A Photographers Place 124
Selima Optique 126
Shamballa 127
Terra Verde 128
Wearkstatt 129

CHINATOWN AND NOLITA

Chinatown

Pearl River Mart 132

Nolita

Calypso St. Barths 133
Charles' Place 135
Daily 235 136
Firefighter's Friend 137
Fresh 138
Housing Works Used
Book Cafe 140
Pop Shop 141

FINANCIAL DISTRICT AND TRIBECA

Financial District

Century 21 144
J & R Computer/
J&R Music World 145
World Collectible Center . . .146

Tribeca

D/L Cerney 147
Oser 148

Stores by category

The following includes the 100 best together with the most interesting stores a short walk away.

BAGS

Il Bisonte 19, 122
Jamin Puech 134
Jutta Neuman 95
Kate Spade 113
Louis Vuitton 116
Manhattan Portage 96

BOOKS

Alabaster Bookstore 100
Books of Wonder 70
Coliseum Books 34
Complete Traveller 47
Corner Bookstore. 20
Crawford Doyle Bookstore ...21
Different Light Bookstore 65
Gotham Book Mart 56
Housing Works 140
Kitchen Arts & Letters 22
Mysterious Bookshop. 51
Oscar Wilde Bookstore 87
Photographers Place 124
Rizzoli Bookstore 49
Shakespeare & Co. 99
Skyline Books and Records ..71
Strand Bookstore. 103
Three Lives & Co 86
Tompkins Square Books ... 103

CHOCOLATE

Fifth Avenue Chocolatière 52
Richart. 53

CIGARS

Nat Sherman 56

CLOTHING-MEN

Abercrombie & Fitch 145
Agnès B Homme. 116
Alberene Cashmeres 43

Albert Sakhai. 65
APC 125
Barneys Co-op 65
Billy Martin's. 17
Calvin Klein 27, 153
Canal Jeans 121
Century 21 144,150
Club Monaco 121
Commes des Garçons 68
Costume National 129
D&G 124
D/L Cerney 147
Daffy's 150
Dave's 65
Diesel 28, 153
DKNY 27
Dolce & Gabbana 24
Emporio Armani 153
Façonnable 62
Firefighter's Friend 137
French Connection 124
Helmut Lang 116
Hotel Venus 118
If 130
Issey Miyake 21
Jeffrey NY 67
Juan Anon 108
Liquid Sky 138
Nicole Farhi 27
99X 97
Nova USA 106
Nylonsquid 138
Old Navy 151
Original Levi's Store 154
Parke & Ronen 68
Paul Smith 85
Prada 24
Primal Stuff 92
Ralph Lauren 24, 154
Savoia 102

Sean .38
Syms 145, 151
T.J. Maxx 151
Ted Baker 130
Timtoum 107
Urban Outfitters 28, 80
Versace 24, 154
X-Large 142
Yohji Yamamoto 130

CLOTHING-WOMEN

Abercrombie & Fitch 145
Agnès B 114
Air Market 97
Alberene Cashmeres 43
Albert Sakhai 65
Anthropologie 119
APC 125
Arlene Bowman 83
Barneys Co-op 65
Betsey Bunky Nini 15
Betsey Johnson 36
Big Drop 124
Bond 07 92
Calvin Klein 27, 153
Calypso St. Barths 133
Carla Berhle 149
Canal Jeans 121
Catherine 111
Century 21 . . . . .144, 150
Chloe 24
Christopher Totman 134
Club Monaco 121
Commes des Garçons 68
Costume National 129
Cynthia Rowley 129
D&G 124
D/L Cerney 147
Daffy's 150
Daryl K. 93
Dave's 65
Diesel 28, 153
DKNY 27
Dolce & Gabbana 24
Dollhouse 19
Dosa 127
Dressing Room 141
Eileen Fisher. 52
Emporio Armani 153
En Soie 20
FAB 208 101
Filene's 150
French Connection 124
Hedra Prue 134
Helmut Lang 116
Hotel Venus 118
If 130
Issey Miyake 21
Jade 136
Jeffrey NY 67
Katayone Adeli 93
Kirna Zabete 116
La Galleria la Rue 76
Label 142
Language 135
Laura Ashley 39
Liquid Sky 138
Loehmann's 150
Marc Jacobs 125
Marcoart 108
Mary Adams 107
Mayle 137
Miu Miu 125
Naked Ape 98
Nicole Farhi 27
No XS 101
Nova USA 106
Nylonsquid 138
Old Navy 151
Olive & Bette's 37
Original Levi's Store 154
Parke & Ronen 68
Prada 24
Primal Stuff 92
Pucci 19
Ralph Lauren 24, 154
Scoop 16, 121
Soho Woman on the Park 59
SSS Nice Price 60
Steven Alan 126
Syms 145, 151
T.J. Maxx 151
TG-170 106
Timtoum 107
Tocca 125
Todd Oldham 127
Tracy Feith 135
Tse Cashmere 24

Urban Outfitters 28, 80
Versace 24, 154
Vivienne Tam 114
Xuly Bët 108
Yohji Yamamoto 130
Zara International 28, 120

COLLECTIBLES

Alphaville 78
Dollhouse Antics 19
Forbidden Planet 104
Jerry Ohlinger's Movie 84
Rita Ford Music Boxes 19
Second Childhood 79
Somethin' Else! 68
Tender Buttons. 27
World Collectible Center . . .146

CONSIGNMENT STORES

Allan & Suzi 32
Fan Club 71
INA .117
Tokio 7 101

COSTUMES

Adventure Shop 100
Albert Sakhai 65

DEPARTMENT STORES

Barneys Co-op 65
Barneys New York 26
Bergdorf Goodman 51, 151
Bloomingdale's 28, 151
Century 21 . . . . .144, 150
H&M 153
Henri Bendel 51, 151
Loehmann's 150
Lord & Taylor 43, 152
Macy's 61, 152
Old Navy 151
Pearl River Mart 132
Saks Fifth Avenue 45, 152
Shanghai Tang 26
Takashimaya 61, 152
Zitomer 30, 152

ELECTRONICS AND
GADGETS

As Seen On TV 45

B&H Photo-Video 46
Hammacher Schlemmer 29
J&R Computer 145, 150
Sony Style Store 53, 154

EROTICA

Body Worship 103
Condomania 84
Eve's Garden 48
Naughty and Nice 32
Pleasure Chest 86

FABRICS AND HOME SEWING

Barsouv 105
Beckenstein Men's 105
Hersh Button 55
Kaarta's Imports 41
Kinnu 139
Tender Buttons 27

FOSSILS AND BONES

Maxilla & Mandible 36

GAMES

Dart Shoppe 74
Village Chess Shop 88

GARDEN

Chelsea Garden Center 82
Grass Roots Garden 115

GIFTS

ABC Carpet & Home 69
Ad Hoc Softwares 123
Adrien Linford 30
Aero 115
African Paradise 41
Air Market 97
Alphabets 90
Avventura 35
Bond 07 92
Daily 235 136
Delphinium 58
E.A.T. Gifts 21
Eclectic Home 67
Exit 9 91
FarFetched 100
Felissimo 50
Firefighter's Friend 137

H 95
Hudson Dry Goods 35
Hudson Street Papers 83
Indians on Columbus 37
It's a Mod, Mod World 92
Kate's Paperie 119
Knobkerry 148
Language 135
MacKenzie-Childs 23
Marcoart 108
Mxyplyzyk 85
Nicolina 57
Only Hearts 39
Pop Shop 141
Reminiscence 75
Sears and Robot 102
Serendipity 3 18
Shi 137
Somethin' Else! 68
Terra Verde 128
Tink 108
Urban Outfitters 28, 80
Vinnie's Tampon Case 109
XYZ Total Home 73
Zona 114

GLOVES

La Crasia a.k.a Glove Street . .53

HATS

Amy Downs 106
The Hat Shop 116
Kelly Christy 137
Manny's Millinery 54
Shoofly 35

HOUSEWARES AND HOME ACCESSORIES

ABC Carpet & Home 69
Ad Hoc Softwares 123
Adrien Linford 30
Aero 115
Amalgamated Home 87
Anthropologie 119
Avventura 35
Bath Island 34
Bed Bath & Beyond 150
Bedford Downing 64
Bond 07 92

Broadway Panhandler 111
Candleschtick 64
Central Carpet 85
Delphinium Home 58
Dish Is 64
Dom 118
Eclectic Home 67
En Soie 20
Exit 9 91
Fishs Eddy 72
H 95
Hudson Dry Goods 35
It's a Mod, Mod World 92
Jonathan Adler 112
Just Bulbs 73
Knobkerry 148
La Tienda Rancho 139
Lancelotti Housewares 90
Language 135
Laytner's Linen 33
MacKenzie-Childs 23
Michael Anchin Glass 137
Mxyplyzyk 85
New York Cake & Baking 65
Nicolina 57
Oser 148
Our Name is Mud 86
Potala 46
Quilted Corner 99
Restoration Hardware 69
Shi 137
Terra Verde 128
Tink 108
Tocca 125
Transitions 96
Urban Outfitters 28, 80
XYZ Total Home 73
Zabar's Kitchen Store 33
Zona 114

JEWELRY AND WATCHES

Amle Arte 37
Cartier 53
Charles' Place 135
Fragments 113
Home Boy Jewelry 41
Indians on Columbus 37
L'Atelier 92
Push 136

Shamballa 127
Swatch 38
Tiffany & Co 51
Time Will Tell 29

KIDS' STUFF

Alphabets 90
The Ballet Company 33
Big City Kite Co 16
Bombalulu's 81
Books of Wonder 70
Bu and the Duck 148
Calypso Enfants 136
Dollhouse Antics 19
E.A.T. Gifts 21
Enchanted Forest 112
F.A.O. Schwarz 49
Firefighter's Friend 137
Hudson Street Papers 83
Rita Ford Music Boxes 19
Second Childhood 79
Shoofly 35
Wicker Garden's Children 20

KIMONOS

Kimono House 103

LINGERIE

Enelra 101
Le Corset 121
Only Hearts 39

MAKEUP AND BEAUTY

Aphrodisia 79
Aveda 122
Elizabeth Arden 62
Face Stockholm 114
Fresh 138
Kiehl's 96
M.A.C 87, 113
Origins 119
Sephora 120, 154

MARKETS

Annex Flea 63
Orchard Street Market 105
Soho Antique Fair 130
Spring Street Market 115

MUSEUM STORES

Am. Museum of Natural History ..40
Guggenheim Museum 120
Library Shop 57, 59
Lower East Side Tenement ..105
Metropolitan Museum of Art .114
Museum Company 62
Museum of Modern Art 62
Pierpont Morgan Library 47
Studio Museum of Harlem ...41

MUSICAL EQUIPMENT

Manny's Music 55

OPTICIANS

Oliver Peoples 119
Selima Optique 126
Sol Moscot Opticians 104

PETS

Doggie-Do and Pussycats Too! ..48
Karen's for People and Pets ..17
Le Chien 28

PHARMACIES

Bigelow Chemist 80
Cambridge Chemists 18
Lascoff Pharmacy 17
Thompson Chemists 117
Zitomer 30, 152

PLASTIC

Industrial Plastics 133

QUILTS

Quilted Corner 99
Susan Parrish Antiques 84

RECORDS

Academy Records and CDs ..70
Dancetracks. 92
Footlight Records 94
J&R Music World 145, 150
Jazz Record Center 66
Other Music 98
Skyline Books & Records 71
Timtoum 107
Tompkins Square Books 103
Virgin Megastore 155

SAMPLE SALES

SSS Nice Price 60

SHAVING EQUIPMENT

Art of Shaving 44

SHOES

E. Vogel 138
French Sole 15
Jimmy Choo 53
Jutta Neuman 95
Kirna Zabete 116
Manolo Blahnik 51
Medici Shoes 76
99X .97
Otto Tootsi Plohound 123
Peter Fox Shoes 117
Shoofly 35
Sigerson Morrison 134
Stephane Kelian 125

SHOPPING MALLS

Manhattan Mall 61
Trump Tower 51
World Trade Center 147

SPORTS

Niketown 153
Oser 148
Paragon Sporting Goods 74
Polo Sport 119
Prada Sport 129
Reebok 38

STATIONERY AND ART

Art Store 93
Hudson Street Papers 83
Il Papiro 15
Ink Pad 68
Kate's Paperie 119
Lincoln Stationers 34
Ordning & Reda 38
Paper Access 71
Papivore 86
Pearl Paint 133
Sam Flax 72

THEME STORES

Disney 153
Warner Brothers 155

UMBRELLAS

Uncle Sam 49

VIDEOS

J&R Music World 145, 150
Virgin Megastore 155

VINTAGE AND ANTIQUE-CLOTHING

Anna 91
Apartment 141 97
Cherry 108
Darrow 72
Fab 208 101
Metropolis 97
1909 Company 122
Oser 148
Quilted Corner 99
Reminiscence 75
Resurrection 100
Screaming Mimi 99
Stella Dallas 88
Timtoum 107
Transitions 96
What Goes Around 119

VINTAGE & ANTIQUE-GENERAL

Cherry 108
Cobblestones 96
Out of the Closet 25
Quilted Corner 99
Susan Parrish Antiques 84

WEDDINGS

Mary Adams 107
Tati .57
Vera Wang Bridal House 21
Wearkstatt 129

WIGS

Mona Hair Center 40

WITCHCRAFT

Candle Therapy 33

Introduction

New York City at street level is as mesmerizing as any place in the world. The folks parading the sidewalks contribute to the never-ending procession of diversity, as do the bars and restaurants. But can you imagine what Manhattan would look like without its off-beat and colorful storefronts? If every store were a GAP or a Banana Republic wouldn't the island suddenly look dull? The oftentimes eccentric little stores which line the blocks of the city are as varied, amusing, and individualistic as any of its inhabitants. It's these fascinating places which you'll find described in the following pages.

When I first arrived here from England, I landed some work writing about stores for *Time Out New York* magazine. I got to know the city, not neighborhood by neighborhood, but store by store. I confess, stores are my landmarks and touchstones in much the way that the Brooklyn Bridge or the Empire State Building are for others. Still, you can't write elegant and engaging prose if you don't have something good to write about. Thankfully, New York has the greatest concentration of amazing, one-of-a-kind stores in the world.

In case you were wondering exactly what constitutes a great "little store," here are my criteria:

- The store must be unique, not a chain. It might have one or two other locations, but you certainly won't find one in every mall in America.

- The store has managed to retain its own personality and niche, despite increasing competition from generic, cookie-cutter chains.

- "Little" doesn't refer to square footage (although in space-starved New York City, most stores are relatively small), it refers to an intimate approach. The items in the store must be selected with great care and consideration, and the staff must be kind and courteous.
- You could visit, not buy anything, and still have a great time just browsing.

Of course this guide is, by nature, highly selective. It would be impossible to mention every little store in the city, and as a result I've had to make some tough choices. You should also note that all furniture and food stores have been excluded by design; the sheer numbers of these stores warrant separate guide books. Similarly, for the sake of concision, this guide covers Manhattan and not the other boroughs. In spite of the high degree of selectivity, if you visit every place mentioned in this book, you'll not only wear out the soles on your sneakers (time to buy new ones!), you'll also visit just about every neighborhood in Manhattan. Happy shopping...

HOW TO USE THIS BOOK

The stores are organized for you by neighborhoods, and they're in alphabetical order. Following each main entry you'll find a section entitled "while you're there..." Here you'll find a list of a few of the most interesting stores within a three-block radius. Visitors to New York City can use this section to make sure they don't miss out on the better-known and bigger-name stores. The big department, specialty and discount stores are to be found in the appendices.

To find an excellent jazz record store or a handmade paper emporium, use the category contents (see pg. 6). And there's an alphabetical listing of all the stores too.

Upper East Side

FOR MOST FOLKS, SHOPPING ON THE UPPER EAST SIDE (above 57th Street, east of Central Park) means a single avenue: Madison. Between 60th and 72nd Streets, you'll find every big name from Armani and Versace to Calvin Klein and Ralph Lauren. Don't fixate: there are plenty of interesting stores to be found on the side streets and nearby avenues. While you're in the neighborhood, don't forget to check out the museum stores: the Metropolitan Museum of Art, the Guggenheim, Cooper-Hewitt, the Frick, the Whitney and the Jewish Museum, all have particularly good gift stores.

Betsey Bunky Nini

980 Lexington Avenue bet. 71st and 72nd Streets
744-6716

When three gal pals Betsey, Bunky, and Nini opened a clothing boutique on 53rd Street back in 1969, they wanted to provide women with the best of the new, progressive, gorgeous women's clothing. Although the original owners have long since moved on to other ventures (Betsey is clothing designer Betsey Johnson), the store still lives on, as does its original mission.

Under a single roof you'll find racks brimming with at least 2,000 garments by a diverse range of American and European designers. High-end labels like Alberta Ferretti keep company with lesser known names like California designer Peter Cohen, and cult brands like English Eccentrics. The look is feminine and tailored, but not in any boring and traditional sense. Everything is blessed with interesting details and an unusual edge. You'll find some scarves, but no shoes or purses. Expect lots of cashmere sweaters in winter and a great range of T-shirts in summer. Prices are mid-to-high range.

While you're there...

French Sole, 985 Lexington Avenue bet. 71st and 72nd Streets, 737-2859 • Slip-on, ballet-style slippers are the order of the day at French Sole, a store that does one thing and does it well.

Il Papiro, 1021 Lexington Avenue bet. 73rd and 74th Streets, 288-9330 • Extremely fine Italian stationery products including hand-marbleized papers from Florence and leather bound albums at appropriately precious prices.

Scoop, 1275 Third Avenue bet. 73rd and 74th Streets, 535-5577 • An uptown location for Stephen Greenfield's perfect collection of very cool, mid-priced women's separates. Great accessories and t-shirts too.

Big City Kite Co.

1210 Lexington Avenue at 82nd Street • 472-2623

ig City Kite Co. proves that niche retailing really does work. The only kite store in New York has been selling kites, kites, and nothing but kites since 1963. Pretty remarkable considering that with the exception of Central Park, there's very little space to fly kites in Manhattan.

The tiny store is awash with color. Kites in bright hues are suspended from the ceiling—as many as possible in such a small space. While most folks come here to buy kites to fly, there are those who buy them as decorative objects, especially the beautiful hand-painted Chinese silks. There are kites shaped as animals, professional-looking stunt kites, and carefully constructed box-kites. In recent years, Big City has diversified into other flying toys, including Frisbees and boomerangs. And if your current kite is suffering from a chronic case of the nose dives, bring it in and get some advice from one of the Big City staffers who, pardon the pun, really know their ropes.

While you're there...

Karen's for People and Pets, 1195 Lexington Avenue bet. 80th and 81st Streets, 472-9440 • A pet store that satisfies pet owners as much as their pampered pooches and pussycats. High quality food products, great accessories, and a grooming parlor too.

Lascoff Pharmacy, 1209 Lexington Avenue at 82nd Street, 288-9500 • This cavernous corner-pharmacy has been here since 1899. A full range of beauty products and pharmaceuticals are carried.

Billy Martin's

220 East 60th Street bet. Second and Third Avenues
861-3100

*I*f John Voight striding down Fifth Avenue to the tune of Nilsson in *Midnight Cowboy* is your idea of ultimate style, you'd better head straight for Billy Martin's. Who knew the late, one-time Yankees manager had a fetish for the Wild West? This mini-theme store, which Martin opened in 1977, recently moved its location from Madison Avenue to 60th Street, but it's still packed with Western gear, all of the highest quality. Complementing the hardwearing cowboy shirts and chunky silver belt buckles are turquoise and silver jewelry, suede fringed jackets, and the softest rugs and blankets by Native American and Southwestern artists. The store offers a custom cowboy boot service, but be forewarned that these beautifully crafted items don't come cheap. Folks seeking ten gallons that fit perfectly can have their heads measured for size. At the back of the space you'll even find an in-store saloon.

Those playing at Midnight Cowboys and Indians should take note—liquor is not for sale.

While you're there...

Serendipity 3, 225 East 60th Street bet. Second and Third Avenues, 838-3531 • The legendary restaurant (famous for their frozen hot chocolate) has its own gift-store attached, filled with kids' toys and kooky gifts.

Cambridge Chemists

21 East 65th Street at Madison Avenue • 734-5678

Sometimes you get sick-not sick enough to warrant a trip to the doctor-but sick enough to make getting to work feel like climbing Mount Everest. That's when you need a friendly, reliable pharmacy just like Cambridge Chemists. Since it first opened its doors in 1941, this European-style chemist has been administering prescriptions and advice to Upper East Siders. Inside, Cambridge's wood and glass cabinets have turned in an even longer tour of duty—they were bought from another, older pharmacy and clock in at a little over a century. Even the service here harks back to a gentler age. Cambridge's pharmacists and staff, who still compound some prescription pills by hand, are almost too polite to be real.

The pharmacy excels in its enormous range of imported items, unrivaled in the neighborhood—everything from British flu remedies to Italian hair products. Whatever ails you—be it jet-lag, pimples, or backache-the staff can recommend some kind of cure. Cambridge is also one of the few places in New York where you'll find John Bull, the potpourri perfume which was made for infamous Vogue editor Diana Vreeland. The scent was a favorite of one of the neighborhood's most beloved residents, Jackie O.

While you're there...

Rita Ford Music Boxes, 19 East 65th Street bet. Madison and Fifth Avenues, 535-6717 • One of the city's most unique specialty stores, Rita Ford sells music boxes, both new and antique, and not much else (besides CDs of music box music). Repairs a specialty.

Il Bisonte, 22 East 65th Street bet. Madison and Fifth Avenues, 717-4771 • Fine Italian leather bags, purses and wallets in hard wearing, classic shapes and sizes.

Pucci, 24 East 64th Street bet. Madison and Fifth Avenues, 752-4777 • Emilio Pucci's legendary psychedelic designs are represented here in all their colorful glory. There's a good range of silk capri pants, which Pucci claims to have invented.

Dollhouse Antics

1343 Madison Avenue at 94th Street • 876-2288

*I*f you ever wondered what it would feel like to be Gulliver in Lilluput, take a tour of Dollhouse Antics. Nothing here is more than a foot high, although much is less than an inch.

While this is not a place for the farsighted, the store has

the very best miniatures and miniature houses in the city: There are dinky coffee pots, and four-poster beds just big enough for a flea, teeny Beatles albums, impossibly small chess sets, and microscopic Fig Newtons. Fine reproductions of furniture, figures, and other trinkets would be awe-inspiring enough if they were real size. In their shrunken form, they're truly amazing. Fully-electrified toy houses are so well-appointed they'll probably put your own pad to shame. While some of the more complex items sell for hundreds of dollars, there are, thankfully, little things to be found here for just a few bucks. The store also does a roaring trade in single dollhouse "gift rooms," which can be "themed" to suit the recipient.

While you're there...

Wicker Garden's Children, 1327 Madison Avenue bet. 93rd and 94th Streets, 410-7001 • If you're having a baby or going to a baby shower, stop by Wicker Garden for exquisite imported kids' clothes and nursery necessities.

The Corner Bookstore, 1313 Madison Avenue at 93rd Street, 831-3554 • A friendly neighborhood bookstore featuring a good range of books for kids and Murphy the cat, the store's mascot.

En Soie

988 Madison Avenue at 77th Street • 717-7958

ou might well recognize En Soie's distinctive patterned silks and cottons. Take the chic design on an Hermes scarf, add the charming touch of a Tin-Tin illustration, and you're somewhere near. In the 50s, couturiers such as Dior, Balengciaga, Schiaparelli and Givenchy adored En Soie's luxurious silks, using them to make some of their most impressive creations.

The company with the "dancing rabbits" logo, which was founded in 1910 in Zurich, Switzerland, got its start supplying fabrics to Europe and beyond. While these days you can shop for En Soie's jewel-colored silks and cottons by the yard (at this, their only New York store), there's another good reason to visit. Since 1986, designer Ines Boesch has been creating a women's line entirely from En Soie fabrics. Her delectable, handcrafted creations will often hark back to the 50s silhouettes which suit En Soie fabrics so well. Also to be found here are porcelain items decorated with distinctive swirls, as well as pretty silk pillows, purses, and other accessories. Look for the photo of Audrey Hepburn circa 1955 at the back of the store—she's dressed head to toe in Givenchy made from En Soie fabrics.

While you're there...

Issey Miyake, 992 Madison Avenue at 77th Street, 439-7822 • An uptown location for the avant-garde designer's clothing for in inventive fabrics and ground-breaking shapes.

Vera Wang Bridal House, 991 Madison Avenue at 77th Street, 628-3400 • The modern bride would be at sea without Vera Wang's clean-lined solutions to wedding day frothiness.

E.A.T. Gifts, 1062 Madison Avenue bet. 80th and 81st Streets, 861-2544 • A one-of-a-kind gift store with an abundance of toys, children's books, greeting cards, tableware, trinkets and treasures.

Crawford Doyle Bookstore, 1020 Madison Avenue bet. 81st and 82nd Streets, 288-6300 • A genuine neighborhood bookstore that's literary without being intimidating. Especially good for books on New York.

Kitchen Arts & Letters

1435 Lexington Avenue bet. 93rd and 94th Streets

876-5550

I grew up in a house where mealtimes were sacred, where food was prepared with love and attention, and where cooking wasn't just a biological necessity—it was an act of faith. So I'm never happier than when perusing the shelves at Kitchen Arts & Letters. This is the largest store in the country devoted to books on food and wine—it boasts over 10,000 titles in stock including a huge inventory of out-of-print and hard-to-find books.

Owner Nach Waxman, a book lover and gourmand, keeps the store well-supplied with all the latest cookbooks (some of them hot off the press in publisher's galley form). He has imports from the world over, but he also prides himself on selectivity. Only quality contributions to food and wine literature are here, which probably pleases the store's customers, a good percentage of whom are professional chefs, food writers, and cooking teachers.

Worth noting is that since the store opened in 1983, Waxman has chosen to supply only one item of kitchen equipment and one cooking ingredient: a yogurt cheese strainer and extra virgin olive oil from Nice.

MacKenzie-Childs

824 Madison Avenue at 69th Street
570-6050

The MacKenzie-Childs store—from the outside, a kind of cross between a gingerbread house and a circus tent—is a fish out of water next to sleek neighbors, Versace and Prada. Artists Victoria and Richard MacKenzie-Childs, who are justly famous for their colorful, hand-painted majolica tableware, created this elaborate and whimsical store to house their handmade ceramics, tiles, linens, glassware, floor coverings, lamps, fabrics, trims, and all manner of interesting gift items and home accessories.

Inside, you can wander at your leisure around the townhouse space which covers various levels, corridors, and cubbyholes. Floors are handpainted with jacquards and checks, stairways are lined with twisting tree trunks, the upstairs tearoom is covered in a mosaic made of mirrors, cabinet doors are daubed with tree bark, walls are covered with murals, and, in one room, pasta shells and lentils supplant wallpaper. Prices are often high, but the goods are of the highest quality. Children love this store, not least for the miniature mansion exhibit upstairs—a stunning dollhouse which is so awe-inspiring, it even justifies the admission fee to see it. You'll find another, less extravagant, location for MacKenzie-Childs along the block at 940 Madison Avenue at 74th Street.

While you're there...

Gianni Versace, 815 Madison Avenue bet. 68th and 69th Streets, 744-6868 • Two floors of outlandish fashion—one for women and one for men, housed in the former Vanderbilt mansion, which the late designer had decorated with lavish mosaics.

Dolce & Gabbana, 825 Madison Avenue bet. 68th and 69th Streets, 249-4100 • Dress up like a 50s Italian film star at the Italian design duo's marvelous flagship store.

Tse Cashmere, 827 Madison Avenue at 69th Street, 472-7790 • Another flagship—Tse has handknits and accessories in softest cashmere, and in every color.

Prada, 841 Madison Avenue at 70th Street, 327-4200 • Many urban dwellers think a wardrobe without Prada is like a night without stars. This store holds the entire Prada universe—shoes, clothing, and accessories for men and women. In midtown, see the new and biggest Prada store at 724 Fifth Avenue bet. 56th and 57th Streets, 664-0010; and their shoe store at 45 East 57th Street bet. Park and Madison Avenues, 308-2332.

Chloe, 850 Madison Avenue at 70th Street, 717-8220 • This 3,000 square foot flagship is filled with the French fashion house's elegant designs, currently created by Stella McCartney.

Ralph Lauren, 867 Madison Avenue bet. 71st and 72nd Streets, 606-2100 • Housed in the old Rhinelander mansion, the Lauren flagship is as famous for its English country castle setting as its complete line of Ralph Lauren and Polo.

Out of the Closet

220 East 81st Street bet. Second and
Third Avenues • 472-3573

*A*nyone who longs for the genuine excitement of thrift store shopping, but is dissatisfied with what's available in the city, needs to know about Out of the Closet. New York's first AIDS thrift store benefits over 50 charities every year. The store boasts 10,000 books, 3,000 records, and more bric-a-brac, artwork, crafts, and antiques than any other thrift store in New York. It's also a great place to find vintage garb for men, which is often in short supply at most vintage clothing stores.

Out of the Closet, which is run by volunteers, is regularly inundated with generous donations, so you never know what you might turn up here. The store once sold a plate decorated by Picasso, and its most expensive item to date was a Boudin painting priced at $19,000. Conversely, you can pick up a pair of Levi's here for under $20. Even the building which houses the store is of interest—an 1840s farmhouse and stable. Bear in mind that Out of the Closet is closed in August.

Shanghai Tang

714 Madison Avenue bet. 63rd and 64th Streets
888-0111

Although Shanghai Tang has moved from its location across from Barneys on Madison Avenue to an elegant five-story townhouse two blocks up, owner and entrepreneur Alan Tang is still providing New Yorkers with his colorful take on Chinese classics. Inside the store, with its deep red brocaded wallpaper and teeny upstairs tearoom, you'll find clothing and accessories that are irreverent variations on time-honored Chinese designs. The racks are filled with Mandarin coats made from finest Chinese silk (in a variety of shades from magenta to electric yellow) and floor length cheung sams in lush, rich-colored velvets. There's clothing for men, women and kids.

Here, both casual and formal, as well as accessories for the person and the home. The fifth floor is home to the store's own tailor. Tang is playing around with his heritage and enjoying it. He loves to make reference to Chinese political icons—a watch shows Chairman Mao saluting, his free arm acting as a second hand. Also here are T-shirts and baseball caps keeping good company with softest silk scarves and snazzy paper lanterns.

While you're there...

Barneys New York, 660 Madison Avenue at 61st Street, 826-8900 • You shouldn't come to New York without experiencing Barneys, whose talented buyers supply the store with the most gorgeous designer clothing and delectable accessories on the planet.

Calvin Klein, 654 Madison Avenue at 60th Street, 292-9000 • A four-floor shrine to clean lines and lack of clutter. This is Klein's flagship, and every aspect of his empire is represented including clothing, footwear, housewares, furniture and those famous undies.

DKNY, 655 Madison Avenue at 60th Street, 223-3569 • Donna Karan's three-level flagship is a stunning showcase for her less expensive, younger clothing and accessories lines.

Nicole Farhi, 14 East 60th Street, 421-7720 • The British-based, French-born designer's store is as elegant as the separates she creates for men and women. The flagship has its own restaurant, cafe, and home accessories department.

Tender Buttons

143 East 62nd Street bet. Lexington and
Third Avenues • 758-7004

Sometimes, the little things in life really do matter—especially at Tender Buttons. Less of a store and more of a button museum, this charming place with the pretty, wooden storefront has been selling lots and lots of beautiful buttons since its doors first opened in 1960.

Precious antique buttons from as early as the 18th century and buttons which have been converted into cufflinks are secured in glass cabinets, but the remainder of the store's inventory is housed in stacks of cardboard cartons. There are buttons in rainbow colors, buttons in wood and rhinestone, plastic and pearl buttons, buttons from far-flung countries, animal-shaped buttons, and silly novelty buttons. One of the delights of a visit to Tender Buttons is reading the wonderful handwritten descriptions of each carton's contents. Here are a few of my favorites: "Mysterious spiral, delicious pink," "Mother of Pearl in bright, lucid colors," "Traditional English Horn—wonderful mottled markings," and "Gummy squares in bright, candy colors." In a store where a humble object is elevated to art, such inadvertent poetry is indeed appropriate.

While you're there...

Le Chien, 1044 Third Avenue at 62nd Street, 752-2120 • The chandelier gives it away—this is the ritziest pet shop and grooming parlor in New York. Accessories, treats, real live pooches, and the store's own pet cologne.

Diesel, 770 Lexington Avenue at 60th Street, 755-9200 • The cult young brand isn't to the taste of everyone, but their enormous and colorful flagship, with its 21st century feel, is a not-to-be-missed shopping experience.

Bloomingdale's, 1000 Third Avenue bet. 59th and 60th Streets, 705-2000 • The world-famous department store, or Bloomie's as it is affectionately known, is so big you can enter on Lexington Avenue, too. Make certain to visit the store's own chocolate factory and Barbie boutique.

Zara International, 750 Lexington Avenue at 59th Street, 754-1120 • An uptown location for the Spanish chain that specializes in very wearable separates for women at work and play. Your best bet if you need something cheap and cheerful, fast.

Urban Outfitters, 127 East 59th Street bet. Lexington and Park Avenues, 688-1200 • An uptown location for the hip housewares and clothing chain. Great for vintage garb and greeting cards too.

Hammacher Schlemmer, 147 East 57th Street bet. Lexington and Third Avenues, 421-9000 • Worth the extra walk for its huge selection of gadgets and games. Established in 1848, HS claims to be the first store to sell the pop-up toaster.

Time Will Tell

962 Madison Avenue bet. 75th and 76th Streets
861-2663 • www.timewilltell.com

Owner Stewart Unger wrote the book on watches—well, a book called American Wristwatches to be precise. His store, with its distinctive black-and-white front, isn't so patriotic. Inside are watches by the major European manufacturers: Patek Phillipe, Rolex, Cartier, and Breitling. In spite of the big name brands and the Madison Avenue address, Time Will Tell has the feeling of a friendly, neighborhood shop. Unger and his knowledgeable staff are on hand to give advice and guide the uninitiated around this tiny store's surprisingly extensive inventory.

The specialty here is antique and vintage watches, some at quite reasonable prices. Once you've held an early 20s Rolex "Oyster" in the palm of your hand, you might find it hard to go back to your disposable Casio. The shop also sells new, less expensive quartz watches in unusual and novelty designs. In addition, Time Will Tell handles repairs, gives appraisals, and will seek out elusive items for collectors. All the watches in the store come with a year-long warranty. And in case you are devoted to things all-American, the store has a fine selection of antique Hamiltons.

While you're there...

Zitomer Pharmacy and Department Store, 969 Madison Avenue bet. 75th and 76th Streets, 737-5560 • The Upper East Side's neighborhood department store is a real oddball, and, consequently, shopping here is a lot of fun. The pharmacy section is particularly extensive.

Adrien Linford, 927 Madison at 74th Street, 628-4500 • A wonderful selection of picture frames, greeting cards, books, tableware, and even a little furniture that makes shopping for holiday gifts a snap.

ꞱꞱpper West Side and Harlem

SHOPPING ON THE UPPER WEST SIDE (above 57th Street, west of Central Park) is simple—stroll up Columbus Avenue from the mid-sixties to the mid-eighties and head back down along Amsterdam; detour to Broadway for the famous food emporiums. Along the route are sidewalk cafes, restaurants, and one-of-a-kind stores. On weekends, visit IS 44 Fleamarket (Columbus Avenue between 76th and 77th Streets). Further uptown, beyond Columbia University, you'll hit historic Harlem's legendary main drag, 125th Street. Concentrated between Lenox and Eighth Avenues are chains such as Old Navy, HMV and Disney alongside discount sportswear and jewelry stores and a smattering of places selling African imports. Don't miss the markets; Mart 125 (260 125th Street between Seventh and Eighth Avenues) and the Malcolm Shabazz Harlem Market (Fifth Avenue at 116th Street).

Allan & Suzi

416 Amsterdam Avenue at 80th Street • 724-7445

*I*n a neighborhood where khakis and sweats reign, dynamic duo Allan and Suzi are undaunted-they keep their overstuffed racks filled with gently-worn designs for men and women by Versace, Jean Paul Gaultier, Moschino, and anyone else with a penchant for glamour. In need of crushed velvet platforms? Sequined hipsters? Rhinestone-studded tube-tops? If you shop for an outfit at Allan & Suzi, you'd better come with a whole lot of attitude (no wonder the store is a favorite with the city's drag queens).

Owners Allan and Suzi, sporting wild white hair and curly red locks respectively, are always on hand to help you find the Dolce & Gabbana that fits. Sing along to some jazz standard as you try on for size, and dance around to make sure you won't fall out of that skimpy Gaultier. The pair's hysterical public access show, in which Allan and Suzi present models wearing clothes from the store, plays constantly on the in-store TV. Although no longer on the air, their show may be revived some-time in the near future, perhaps by the time you read this.

While you're there...

Naughty & Nice, 212 West 80th Street bet. Broadway and Amsterdam Avenues, 787-1212 • An upscale erotic emporium selling fancy lingerie, exotic massage oils, and lots and lots of sex toys.

Candle Therapy, 213 West 80th Street bet. Broadway and Amsterdam Avenues, 260-9188 • Candles and incense and spell-kits and potions-these are a few of this witchcraft store's favorite things.

Laytner's Linen and Home, 2270 Broadway bet. 80th and 81st Streets, 724-0180 • A big general store for the home. There's everything for your fun and stylish urban apartment.

Zabar's Kitchen Store, 2245 Broadway at 80th Street, 787-2000 • After you've shopped for groceries at this famous, less-expensive-than-you-think gourmet emporium, try the kitchenware store upstairs.

The Ballet Company

1887 Broadway bet. 62nd and 63rd Streets
246-6893

As a dance-devoted child, I lived and breathed for my Saturday ballet class. The Ballet Company is the kind of place that once-upon-a-time would have made me weak at the knees. I still feel a little wobbly to this day.

Just around the corner from Lincoln Center, where the American Ballet Theater has its permanent home, the other Ballet Company puts the emphasis on beautiful things for young girls: tutus dotted with embroidered roses, softest velvet leotards, and crystal-covered tiaras. This store also has the city's best range of hard-to-find ballet books and videos, plus a good selection of ballet music on CD. Also worth seeking out are gifts for dance fans, such as Degas-decorated purses and miniature slippers. In the window, and lining the walls of the store, are the toe shoes and slippers (all for sale) that once belonged to famous dancers; alongside are signed photos of prima ballerinas like Gelsey Kirkland and Darcy Kissler, as well as Rudolph Nureyev.

While you're there...

Lincoln Stationers, 1889 Broadway at 63rd Street, 459-3500 • Two floors of pens, paper, binders, books, and other good things for improving the state of affairs at desk-level.

Coliseum Books, 1771 Broadway at 57th Street, 757-8381• This excellent general bookstore is worth the extra walk for its great selection and discounted titles.

Bath Island

469 Amsterdam Avenue bet. 82nd and 83rd Street
787-9415 • www.citysearch.com/nyc/bath island

*I*f your idea of heaven is a candle-lit bathroom, a glass of wine, and a steaming tub overflowing with bubbles, then Bath Island is your Nirvana. This neighborhood fixture has a thousand good things for the bath and bathroom: things to put in the bath and around the bath, shower curtains, loofahs, toothbrushes, bubble bath, essential oils, soap dishes, and the soap to put in them. The store even has spray cleaners for keeping the bathtub and tiles spruce.

You don't go to Bath Island for just those bathroom

essentials, however. You go for the store's excellent custom "scenting services." Get the accomplished "noses" at Bath Island to help mix up the essential oils of your choice. Combine roses with raspberry, lilac with mango, vanilla with jasmine, or any number of other combinations. When you've settled on your personalized scent, have it added to Bath Island's plain bubble baths, moisturizers, shampoos, and even shaving gel.

While you're there...

Shoofly, 465 Amsterdam Avenue bet. 82nd and 83rd Streets, 580-4390 • An uptown location for this store selling imported kids' shoes, hats, and other accessories, with a kid-friendly staff.

Avventura, 463 Amsterdam Avenue at 82nd Street, 769-2510 • A gift store specializing in elaborate ceramics, tableware, and colorful glassware from America and Europe.

Hudson Dry Goods

112 West 72nd Street at Columbus Avenue
579-7397

A warning: Hudson Dry Goods is the kind of home furnishings store that makes you want to throw out the entire contents of your apartment and start over. Well-worn architectural details, such as the mirrors from old cabinet doors and stained glass windows, keep company with brand new sprightly pillows, scented candles, luxurious rugs, and the softest linens. Everything here is hand-selected and displayed in a homey context.

You might unearth classic vintage fans, tin lanterns from Morocco, or handpainted Chinese parasols. At the back of the store are beauty and personal care products, Italian soaps, essential oils, and antique bathroom cabinets. A kind of small-scale, uptown ABC Carpet and Home, that yields just as many good things for your pad as it does great gifts for friends. A new location for Hudson Dry Goods at 873 Broadway between 18th and 19th Streets, 228-7143, has great couches and tables too.

While you're there...

Betsey Johnson, 248 Columbus Avenue, 362-3364 • An uptown location for Betsey Johnson's eternally girlish clothing.

Maxilla & Mandible

451 Columbus Avenue bet. 81st and 82nd Streets
724-6173

*I*t sounds spooky on paper-a store devoted to selling bones, both animal and human-but Maxilla & Mandible doesn't have cobwebs hanging from the ceiling. This elegant (and sanitary) store caters mainly to artists and interior designers who use the bones in still lifes or as decorative pieces. Parents who want a quick natural history fix for the kids often bypass the nearby Natural History Museum and come here instead.

At M & M you can shop for a human knee bone, a turtle skull, or a muskrat skeleton. You might not usually think of a human vertebrae or a wildebeest skull as beauty incarnate, but who could resist the awe-inspiring, intricate curves of a rattlesnake skeleton? Ever seen a raccoon's penis bone? The store also has beautiful, and in some cases valuable, fossils and dinosaur bones. There are sea shells, dried bugs, butterflies, and rocks here as well. The items are well-labeled, so you'll know that the dinosaur's tooth you're looking at is actually 100 million years old. And everything here—yes, even the human bones, culled from the cadavers used by medical schools—is the real thing (don't be spooked).

While you're there...

Amle Arte, 455 Columbus Avenue bet. 81st and 82nd Streets, 501-9577 • Simple, strong, silver jewelry set with colorful semi-precious gemstones by Elma Blints.

Indians on Columbus, 452 Columbus Ave bet. 81st and 82nd Streets, 769-4516 • Traditional and modern, fine art and jewelry by Native American artists.

Olive & Bette's

252 Columbus Avenue bet. 71st and 72nd Streets
579-2178 • www.oliveandbettes.com

ashion-hound Stacey Pecor has been bringing downtown fashion to uptown denizens since 1996. Her two boutiques, one on the Upper West Side and one on the East, are laden with fun and fresh clothing and accessories for girls of all ages; in fact, you'll often see teenagers and their mothers shopping together at the stores. These tiny spaces, no bigger than a couple of walk-in closets, are always packed with great solutions as to what to wear, season after season. Labels to look for include Earl Jean (denim pieces), Shoshanna Lonstein (floral dresses and undies), Michael Stars (T-shirts) as well as items made especially for the store. The staff are friendly and always ready to offer advice as to which skirt to put with which shirt. They keep a database of the purchasing habits of regular customers and kindly contact them when new merchandise arrives. And if you do live downtown or elsewhere and don't want to make the trek uptown, you can order through the store's mail-order catalog (call 888-767-8475) which features imaginary best friends Olive and Bette wearing the latest designs. You'll find the Upper East Side location for Olive & Bette's at 1070 Madison Avenue at 81st Street, 717-9655.

While you're there...

Ordning & Reda, 253 Columbus Avenue bet. 71st and 72nd Streets, 799-0828 • High-quality, brightly colored Swedish stationery (journals, greeting cards and paper) in an all-white setting.

Sean, 224 Columbus Avenue bet. 70th and 71st Street, 769-1489 • A really good bet for fashionable, mid-price men's clothing with a European feel, especially well-tailored shirts.

Swatch, 100 West 72nd Street at Columbus Avenue, 595-9640, www.swatch.com • The complete range of still-fashionable and functional Swatch watch designs.

Reebok, 160 Columbus Avenue bet. 67th and 68th Streets, 595-1480 • All the sweats and sneakers you'll need for working out at Reebok's state of the art sports club next door.

Only Hearts

386 Columbus Avenue bet. 78th and 79th Streets
724-5608

Only Hearts is suspended in a perpetual Valentine's Day. The store is home to heart-shaped soaps and heart-shaped hot water bottles, heart-shaped ice-cube trays and heart-shaped picture frames, and even a heart-shaped picnic basket (you get the picture). Exceptions to the heart-shaped rule include sensual massage oils and books on love and romance.

In case you're beginning to think that the contents of Only Hearts were just a little too cute, let's get one thing straight. The store has lots and lots of their own-brand lingerie, the wonderfully wearable and feminine Only Hearts line. This is one of only a handful of places in the city where you'll find it. The look is fresh and young without forsaking a certain wholesome sexiness. Favorite fabrics are pretty stretch laces and velvets in ice cream colors, and lots and lots of cotton lycra. But inevitably, the cotton-lycra thongs—which fit to perfection—are stored in, yep, little heart-shaped baskets.

While you're there...

Laura Ashley, 398 Columbus Avenue at 79th Street, 496-5110
• Laura Ashley is Britain's reigning queen of chintz and floral prints. The New York store has fabrics, home-furnishings, and clothing for women and girls.

Museum Shop at the American Museum of Natural History, 79th Street and Central Park West, 769-5150 • Gifts, gadgets, and books devoted to science, history, astronomy, and the wonders of the natural world.

Mona Hair Center

28 West 125th Street bet. Fifth Avenue and
Lenox Avenue • 426-7439

Harlem is famous for many things—its jazz, its gospel choirs, its soul food, its vital atmosphere, and its beautiful brownstones. Add wigs to that list. On this block of 125th Street alone, there must be a dozen wig stores, all of them touting big hair, hairpieces, braids, and bouffants. It's hard to choose between the stores, but I'd say Mona's is certainly one of the biggest, definitely the brightest, and it has an excellent selection.

Once inside this hair supermarket, you won't be allowed to try on anything without donning a stocking on your head first, but once you do, test drive a fun-colored bob, or attach a crisp pair of bangs. Do the blonde shag or the chestnut buzz cut without losing as much as a strand of your own hair. Try on a sleek number made from real human hair, or settle on a subtle hairpiece to add volume to lank locks. And if wigs aren't really your thing, they can still help you get a feel for that radical new hairstyle you've been tempted to try.

While you're there...

African Paradise, 27 West 125th Street bet. Fifth and Lenox Avenues, 410-5294 • Your best bet for African imports. Shop for carvings, baskets, musical instruments, and rugs.

Kaarta's Imports, 121 West 125th Street bet. Lenox and Seventh Avenues, 866-4062 • Kaarta's has heaps of well-priced, beautiful fabrics from West Africa including "kente" cloth, which translates as "the fabric of kings."

Studio Museum of Harlem Gift Store, 144 West 125th Street bet. Lenox and Seventh Avenues, 864-4500 • Gifts, greeting cards, and crafts in keeping with the Studio's emphasis on African American artists.

Home Boy Jewelry of Harlem, 166 West 125th Street bet. Lenox Avenue, 316-1320 • The best discounted gold jewelry store on 125th Street specializes in fabulous initial rings and name plate necklaces made-to-order.

Midtown

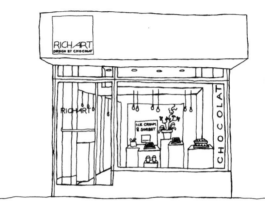

FOR A BUSY COMMERCIAL DISTRICT, Midtown (30th Street to 57th Street) is home to more interesting specialty stores than you might imagine. Of course, the world famous New York department stores (Macy's, Lord & Taylor's, Saks, Bergdorf's, Bendel's) are here. Every major designer and all the chains make appearances. This is the place to find the mega flagships and theme stores. Make certain to head south, below 40th Street on the West Side to the Garment District, where, true to its name, you'll find the best selection of fabrics and notions in the city as well as the discount stores which cluster around the largest department store in the world (otherwise known as Macy's).

Alberene Cashmeres

435 Fifth Avenue bet. 38th and 39th Streets,
2nd floor • 689-0151

C ashmere. Even the word itself sounds lush, soft and...expensive. Thankfully, Alberene Cashmeres keeps a perennial supply of the luxurious stuff at a third less than it would cost in most department stores. America's first specialty cashmere store opened in 1991 after owner Jim Joyner was inspired by a little old cashmere shop he saw in the Burlington Arcade while on vacation in London. Joyner realized that there was a niche to be filled back home.

Joyner keeps his prices down by commissioning and directly importing his cashmere garments from Hawick (pronounced Hoik) in Scotland—which, by the way, is to cashmere what the Champagne region is to champagne. Sweaters, scarves, coats, capes, and gloves in a rainbow of colors are here. If the thought of all the intensive-care involved in owning a cashmere garment gets you down, you can always peruse the fine selection of British teas which Joyner, a self-confessed anglophile, also imports.

While you're there...

Lord & Taylor, 424-434 Fifth Avenue bet. 39th and 40th Streets, 391-3344 • A traditional small town department store in the big city—known for its selection of safe, classic men's and women's wear and main floor cafe.

Art of Shaving

373 Madison Avenue bet. 45th and 46th Streets
986-2905

Who would have thought that the simple act of dragging a razor across your face every morning could be elevated to an art? At Art of Shaving you'll find a devotion to old fashioned grooming that hasn't been seen since the advent of the electric razor.

Macho males who have been longing to pamper themselves but couldn't quite muster the wherewithal, will be relieved to hear that Art of Shaving is a very masculine-looking place, more reminiscent of a fine cigar store than a pampering palace. Dark wood cabinets on the walls house authentic badger brushes from Europe, excellent razors for wet shaving, tubs of shaving soaps, and fine colognes. The store also has other items relating to personal care, such as fancy imported talc, moisturizers, and deodorant.

In the back is an old-fashioned barber shop, where you can get a genuine barber-shop wet shave, as well as more modern spa treatments such as face masks and facial massages. And in case you're tired of Gillette and want to add a little danger to your daily routine, Art of Shaving even sells cut-throat razors—caution advised.

You'll find another location for Art of Shaving at 141 East 62nd Street between Lexington and Third Avenues, 317-8436.

While you're there...

Saks Fifth Avenue, 611 Fifth Avenue bet. 49th and 50th Streets, 753-4000 • The name seems as synonymous with New York City as the Empire State Building. As elegant as ever, Saks continues to serve up good things in a legendary setting.

As Seen On TV

401 Fifth Avenue bet. 36th and 37th Streets
679-0728

*S*ee if this scenario sounds familiar. It's late at night, you're unable to sleep. You turn on the TV to try and bore yourself into a slumber and while watching some forgettable made-for-TV movie, you catch a commercial which makes you sit up in your seat. Somehow, in your sleep-deprived state, you manage to convince yourself you can't live without the revolutionary Magic Duster!

If in the morning, by some miracle, you still feel the same way, but don't want to risk mailing your hard-earned dollars for some product sight unseen, you can pay a visit to As Seen on TV. This store sells the products that commercials tell you are "not available in any stores."

In the flesh, such delights as the Brown and Crispy Microwave Bag and the Ginsu Japanese Knife Set look smaller and less impressive than you might expect (it's like catching a glimpse of your favorite celebrity in the street). Still, it's fun to tinker with the aerosol can that's actually a safe, prod at those pasty-pink silicon bra inserts, test drive the ab crunchers, and leave with a smile on your face (or even a magic duster).

While you're there...

Potala, 9 East 36th Street bet. Madison and Fifth Avenues, 251-0360 • A store selling Tibetan artifacts, books, and incense, that doubles as a travel agency specializing in flights to Asia.

B&H Photo-Video and Pro Audio

420 Ninth Avenue bet. 33rd and 34th Streets
444-6635 • www.bhphotovideo.com

*A*t 35,000 square feet, B&H Photo-Video is up there with the biggest "little places to shop" in this book. Recently, the legendary store moved from its cramped location on West 17th Street to a gigantic new headquarters on an entire block of Ninth Avenue, but thankfully, some of the chaos, color, and "only-in-New-York" atmosphere of the 17th Street store has been retained. Famous for the particularly democratic service of its Jewish salesmen (who don't care whether you're Annie Liebowitz or a tourist in need of a disposable camera), the new store has an unrivaled selection of photo and video equipment.

Best of all, the sales help at B&H is plentiful, knowledgeable, and willing to spend as much time as is necessary to help you find what you need. The store is divided into separate departments for photo, video, lighting, digital, darkroom equipment, and film-processing. B&H carries full lines—not just a selection—of absolutely every brand name in the universe. Visitors from all over confirm there's nowhere quite like B&H.

The Complete Traveller

199 Madison Avenue at 35th Street • 685-9007

lame it on Columbus, if you will. Ever since Chris decided to set sail for India, the inhabitants of planet Earth have been stricken with wanderlust. Next time you get seized by a travel bug, take a trip to New York's oldest travel bookstore before setting sail, then, unlike Columbus, you might not end up in the wrong country.

Complete Traveller has a comprehensive selection of guidebooks and maps to help you navigate your way around every pocket of the planet. Besides the standard complement of Fodor's, Let's Go guides, and Rand McNally's, there are plenty of inspiring travelogues and rare and delightful photo books on hand, many of which make great gifts. And don't miss the adjacent store, which houses a collection of beautiful antiquarian travel books. The selection includes rows and rows of faded red Baedecker's and early travelogues. Sometimes, just wandering around such an inspiring place can feel like a vacation in itself.

While you're there...
Pierpont Morgan Library Store, 29 East 36th Street at Madison Avenue, 685-0610 • One of the prettiest museum stores in the city is brimful with good gift ideas, greeting cards, and books. Imported items from Europe are a specialty.

Doggie-Do and Pussycats, Too!

567 Third Avenue at 38th Street • 661-9111

Only in New York—where people just love to spoil their pets—could you imagine a pet store this chic. Swaths of black fabric frame the front window on either side, shiny black tiles adorn the walls, and the floor is done up in red and yellow checks. Once you get over the decor, you'll find a wide array of unique and creative pet treats and accessories. Check out the doggie-sized four-poster beds, stylish pet clothes, rhinestone studded leashes, and bright red raincoats.

Anything here that's not for a pet per se, is for a pet lover: greeting cards, cookie jars, nightlights, and picture frames are all covered with dog and cat motifs. Doggie-Do even has an outdoor garden which can be booked for pet birthday parties (like I said, only in New York), as well as a grooming parlor for pampering that very special pooch or pussycat.

Eve's Garden

119 West 57th Street bet. Sixth and Seventh Avenues, 12th Floor • 757-8651

Century 21 may have the snagged the tag line "New York's best kept secret," but the real holder of this title should be Eve's Garden. Hopefully Eve's will stay a secret. In fact, the city's only women's-oriented sex store thrives on discretion. Hidden away on the twelfth floor of a commercial building just across the street from Carnegie Hall, Eve's is specifically designed to make women feel comfortable about buying sexual paraphernalia. As a rule, men aren't allowed in the store unless they're accompanied by a woman (don't worry, the friendly, all-female staffers aren't that strident—as long as male visitors are sensitive, they won't be turned away). The products—which include vibrators, massage oils, and erotic and educational literature and videos—are all top notch.

Eve's is a brightly lit place with plush pink carpets. Everything is displayed neatly and with clear instructions. Considering that some of the vibrators and massagers look like a technophobe's nightmare, it's probably just as well that owner Dell Williams considers herself an educator as well as a retailer. In fact, Williams, who founded Eve's as a mail-order operation back in the heady days of early 70s feminism, has created a place that feels ahead of its time to this day.

While you're there...

Uncle Sam, 161 West 57th Street bet. Sixth and Seventh Avenues, 582-1976 • The only specialty umbrella store in the city, and in business since 1866. Umbrellas, canes, and custom work to boot.

Rizzoli Bookstore, 31 West 57th Street bet. Fifth and Sixth Avenues, 759-2424 • Behind the Italiante façade is an elegantly appointed, four-floor bookstore. A treat for those who like to shop for books in an unhurried, refined atmosphere and especially good for art, architecture and design books.

F.A.O. Schwarz, 767 Fifth Avenue at 58th Street, 644-9400 • The legendary, gargantuan toy store is still a magical place for children and their adult companions at any time of year, but especially during the holidays.

Felissimo

10 West 56th Street bet. Fifth and Sixth Avenues
247-5656

*A*specialty store with an multicultural, new age feel, Felissimo has managed to retain the feeling of an intimate boutique in spite of its size (five floors!). Enter this newly renovated, pleasurable zone and you'll hear distant African drums or Latin pipes accompanied by the sound of running water issuing forth from one of the Japanese fountains dotted around. There are plants everywhere, and the decor is warm and earthy. Books, scented candles, and handmade papers are at street level. Scale the sweeping, spiral staircase to find unusual home furnishings, crockery, glassware, a smattering of furniture and clothing, as well as all-natural cosmetics and bath products.

On the fourth floor is Felissimo's lofty tearoom, which seems like a million miles from the Fifth Avenue bustle. Order an afternoon "haiku" tea (which arrives complete with a haiku poem). As a bonus, a tarot reader or astrologer is frequently on hand to tell fortunes. And while you probably won't find any bargains here outside of sale-time, you're still likely to leave feeling that Felissimo is felicitous indeed.

While you're there...

Manolo Blahnik, 31 West 54th Street bet. Fifth and Sixth Avenues, 582-3007 • Considered by some (including most of Seventh Avenue's designers) to be the last word in shoes. The Blahnik boutique has its own back garden, and the footwear is mouthwatering, but suitably high in price.

Henri Bendel, 712 Fifth Avenue at 56th Street, 247-1100 • Something of a treat: this one-of-a-kind New York department store is filled with good things. Worth seeking out, especially for divine clothing and accessories. M.A.C. make-up is on the first floor.

Trump Tower, 725 Fifth Avenue bet. 56th and 57th Streets, 832-2000 • A mall in miniature, Donald's pride and joy has a cluster of big name stores and smaller shops (including another Cartier boutique) under one auspicious roof.

Tiffany & Company, 757 Fifth Avenue at 57th Street, 755-8000 • You can't get breakfast here, but you can gaze into glass cases at some of the world's most beautiful baubles. Just being here increases your elegance rating.

Bergdorf Goodman, 754 Fifth Avenue at 58th Street, 753-7300 • There's only one Bergdorf's and, fortunately for us, it's right here in New York. Seven elegant floors of highly desirable clothes, accessories, and shoes, including the major designers, at stratospheric prices (which can drop considerably during sale-time). The top floor has wonderful tabletop items and gifts.

Mysterious Book Shop, 129 West 56th Street bet. Sixth and Seventh Avenues, 765-0900 • Established in 1979, this friendly bookstore specializing in new, used and antique mystery books is housed in a midtown brownstone. A huge range of "Sherlockia" is carried.

Fifth Avenue Chocolatière

510 Madison Avenue bet. 52nd and 53rd Streets
935-5454

*N*ew York is home to every kind of fine chocolate shop. Some are known for their artful French confections or robust Belgian chocolates, others for their particularly delectable truffles, or their elegant packaging. Fifth Avenue Chocolatière stands out from the crowd, not particularly for the taste of its chocolate (although it is very good), but for the manner in which it is sculpted.

Owner John Whalley has made an art of molding chocolate, and the store's mesmerizing window display proves that no request could ever be too outlandish. Chocolate legs nudge pink chocolate pigs; Empire State Buildings are dwarfed by white chocolate snowmen; chocolate cell phones nestle next to bouquets of red chocolate roses. At last count, Whalley had 6,000 molds in stock, but if he doesn't have what you're looking for, never fear, this master chocolatière will cast a mold specially for you (he does a roaring trade in corporate logos and personalized wedding favors). Everything at Fifth Avenue is made from the finest Belgian chocolate, which can be dyed any color of the rainbow. See what you can dream up.

While you're there...

Eileen Fisher, 521 Madison bet. 53rd and 54th Streets, 759-9888 • This flagship store carries the complete line of Fisher's elegant, comfy women's clothing in natural fabrics.

Jimmy Choo, 645 Fifth Avenue at 51st Street, 593-0800 • British shoemaker Jimmy Choo's store is less of a shoe store and more of a shoe salon. Try on slippers and mules for day and night with impossibly skinny heels and pointy toes at high prices.

Cartier, 653 Fifth Avenue at 52nd Street, 308-0840 • The name says it all. Big rocks and beautiful jewels for very deep pockets.

Richart Design et Chocolat, 7 East 55th Street bet. Fifth Avenue and Madison Avenue, 371-9369 • Handmade French chocolates decorated with such exquisite designs, they should be on display in the nearby Museum of Modern Art. Considered by many to be the best chocolates in New York.

Sony Style Store, Sony Plaza, Madison Avenue at 56th Street, 833-8800 • This flagship is great fun—there's camcorders and Playstations to keep technophiles happy for hours. Test drive video games at one of the consoles on the main floor.

La Crasia a.k.a. Glove Street

304 Fifth Avenue bet. 31st and 32nd Streets
594-2223

ince my mother stopped tying my mittens to my coat with a ribbon, I've lost at least one pair of gloves every winter. Fortunately, I can always go to this specialty glove store to replenish my supply. There are gloves at LaCrasia in every cut, color, fabric, and style—navy lambswool mittens hang next to lacy lilac numbers while a rainbow of gloves in softest leather hang next to shiny pink vinyl arm-lengths. The selection of gloves on display has diminished a bit since owners Jay Ruckle and LaCrasia DuChein gave over the front of their space to a tourist-style gift store, but if you don't see what you want, you can always custom-order it. In the past, LaCrasia has made gloves (or should that be a glove) for none other than Michael Jackson.

Ruckle and DuChein are also glove historians. Hidden away at the back of the store is their very own homestyle glove museum. Ask nicely, and you might even get yourself a tour. The displays include gloves from the Elizabethan era as well as a minuscule pair that were made for Tiny Tim.

Manny's Millinery

26 West 38th Street bet. Fifth and Sixth Avenues
840-2235

*T*here are really two Manny's—one for the warmer months and one for the colder ones. A Garment District fixture since the late 40s, this excellent milliner's resource has straws and linens for spring and summer. In fall and winter, the shelves of Manny's brim over with felts and velours. But there are certain items that the store carries all year round—namely the feathers, flowers, ribbons, and veils used for trimming hats. Kept in grey cardboard cartons piled one on top of the other, the lavish ostrich plumes and dapper pheasant feathers cry out to be snuck inside hatbands.

If you do decide to concoct your own creation, Manny's offers a custom service, which means you can have the hat of your choice hand-blocked (shaped with steam) until it fits your head exactly. And if that doesn't inspire you, Manny's has a very good range of well-priced, ready-to-wear hats at the back of the store, as well as the hatboxes and hatpins that go along with them.

While you're there...

Hersh Sixth Avenue Button, 1000 Sixth Avenue bet. 37th and 38th Street, 391-6615 • Opened in 1918, Hersh has all the fabric, buttons, ribbons, and trimmings a home-sewing fanatic could ever want. If it's not here, you won't find it.

Manny's Music

156 West 48th Street bet. Broadway and
Sixth Avenue • 819-0576

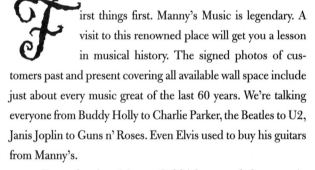

irst things first. Manny's Music is legendary. A visit to this renowned place will get you a lesson in musical history. The signed photos of customers past and present covering all available wall space include just about every music great of the last 60 years. We're talking everyone from Buddy Holly to Charlie Parker, the Beatles to U2, Janis Joplin to Guns n' Roses. Even Elvis used to buy his guitars from Manny's.

From the time Manny Goldrich opened the store in 1935, Manny's has been a big hit with professional musicians, including Charlie Parker and Dizzy Gillespie, who used to hold regular jam sessions upstairs in the store's original location at 48th Street and Sixth Avenue. Manny's provided Ringo with a drum kit for Shea Stadium, sold the Rolling Stones the early fuzz tone they used on "Satisfaction," and restrung the guitars of the world's most famous left-handed guitarist, Jimi Hendrix.

Manny's is still owned and run by the Goldrich family, and they don't rest on their laurels. You'll still find one of the city's best selections of musical instruments, amps, digital recording equipment, and assorted accessories. As is traditional at Manny's, celebrities get the same treatment as any other regular Joe—customer service here is informed and egalitarian.

While you're there...

Gotham Book Mart & Gallery, 41 West 47th Street bet. Fifth and Sixth Avenues, 719-4448 • The walls of this historic bookstore are covered with faded photographs of the authors who have read and shopped here over the years. Best for poetry and literary classics.

Nat Sherman

500 Fifth Avenue at 42nd Street
764-4175 • www.natsherman.com

Since 1930, the Sherman family has been making and selling fine cigars and cigarettes, and their store is now considered a city institution. Current president Joel Sherman, whose father Nat founded the store, continues to produce exceptionally good cigars and the store's own-brand cigarettes, so don't expect to find any old stogies here. Sherman's only sells Partagas, Macanudos, and the store's own brand.

Swing through the revolving doors, and you enter a bygone world of gentlemanly sophistication. Downstairs, attentive staff guide customers around the selections, which are housed in wood and glass cabinets. Upstairs is a walk-in humidor where you'll find smokers' accessories such as ashtrays, cutters, lighters, cases, and antique humidors.

You might notice a framed letter from Humphrey Bogart on the walls, thanking Sherman for his cigars. But as Nat wrote in his private notes on cigarmaking (some of which are published in the store's catalogue): "They're telling me that my cigars are very popular with famous people? Celebrity comes and goes—my cigars will still be around, and they better be great because they'll have my name on 'em."

While you're there...

Tati, 475 Fifth Avenue at 41st Street, 481-TATI • The French bridal superstore is packed with affordable dresses and accessories for brides and bridesmaids to be.

The Library Shop, in the Mid-Manhattan Library, 40th Street and Fifth Avenue, 930-0641 • Like the Library Shop across the street, this little gift store, on the first floor of the Mid-Manhattan Library, is a charming place to buy books, greeting cards, toys and gadgets.

Nicolina

247 West 46th Street bet. Broadway and Eighth
Avenue • 302-NICO

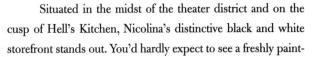

Situated in the midst of the theater district and on the cusp of Hell's Kitchen, Nicolina's distinctive black and white storefront stands out. You'd hardly expect to see a freshly painted white picket fence in midtown Manhattan. What's inside is equally unexpected. In a neighborhood dominated by theaters and restaurants, Nicolina is a one-of-a-kind specialty store selling unique and desirable clothing, accessories and gifts. Owner Nicole Gabrielle scours Europe and America to find very feminine and frequently floral dresses and separates for women as well as unusual hats, bags, jewelry and other accessories. Also here are hand-made baby clothes and toys. There's all manner of gift ideas, including journals, books, picture frames, candles, soaps, jewelry, bath and beauty products. Gabrielle even lines the walls of her store with original artworks for sale, including those of her husband, Ray Gonsalves. The store is open until 8pm in order to catch the theater crowd on their way to dinner and a show. In the breaks between matinees and evening performances, it's not unusual to see actors and actresses stopping by to pick something up. "You never know who's in the dressing room next to you," says Gabrielle. And when you've finished shopping at Nicolina, you can always stop by next door at the Paramount Hotel for a cocktail.

While you're there...

Delphinium, 358 West 47th Street bet. Eighth and Ninth Avenues, 333-7732 • More greeting cards than you know people to send them to at this fun store filled with stationery, candles, gifts and bath accessories. Make time to walk over to **Delphinium Home** at 653 Ninth Avenue bet. 45th and 46th Streets, 957-6928; for great "Pottery Barn-esque" accessories.

Soho Woman on the Park

32 West 40th Street bet. Fifth and Sixth Avenues

391-7263

As many clothing designers seem to forget, women come in various shapes and sizes. Fortunately, Penny Healy hasn't been so remiss. Her store, Soho Woman on the Park, has elegant, wearable clothing in all sizes-including regular sizes 4 to 12 and fuller figure sizes 14 to 24.

Soho Woman on the Park, which relocated from Soho to Bryant Park in 1996 (hence the hybrid name), features a mix of clothing by Healy and other designers from Europe and America. A former Bloomingdale's buyer, Healy loves earthy colors, lush textures, and natural fabrics (such as silks and linen), as do her faithful customers. While her signature "soft dressing" is certainly comfy, it's far from frumpy.

Soho Woman is dotted over with hats, scarves and jewelry to complement bias-cut skirts, Japanese-inspired jackets, and floaty silk-chiffon blouses. Healy also hand-knits sweaters in hand-dyed English yarn, chenille, ribbon, and rope. So when you decide that slavish devotion to fashion is out and quality clothing is in, this is the place to come.

While you're there...

The Library Shop, 455 Fifth Avenue at 40th Street, 340-0839 • Across the street from the Mid-Manhattan Public Library is this store selling unusual, enlightening, and enlivening gifts, books, toys and greeting cards.

SSS Nice Price

261 West 36th Street bet. Seventh and Eighth Avenues, 2nd Floor • 947-8748

Everyone in New York loves a sample sale and with very good reason: The seasons slip by only too quickly, each one bringing with it more wonderful designs and more talented designers. The sample sale is how you and your bank account keep up with the latest trends. Unfortunately, the city's sample sales can be a tough ticket. Some are by invitation only, while others you'll only find out about if you're on a special mailing list. You can also scour the listings in local magazines (*Time Out New York* is a good bet).

SSS Nice Price is your other solution. A permanent fixture in the garment district, this is where designers send their samples and rejects when they don't want to hold a sale themselves. Hidden away in a commercial building, the weekly sales feature three or four womenswear designers at a time. Call the hotline to find out who's selling this week. Designers who regularly sell here include Donna Karan, Calvin Klein, Cynthia Rowley, Betsey Johnson, and Marc Jacobs.

The only drawback, as with regular sample sales, is that there are no changing rooms. But that doesn't stop the determined shoppers who frequent Nice Price. They strip off down to their undies in full view to ascertain whether that $120 barely-there, puce-colored Versace dress is really the bargain it appears to be.

While you're there...

Macy's, 151 West 34th Street bet. Sixth and Seventh Avenues, 695-4400 • The biggest department store in the world has everything in the world and then some. Top designers, store brands, electronics, food, home furnishings and much more are all here under one enormous roof.

Manhattan Mall, Sixth Avenue bet. 33rd and 34th Streets • You don't come to New York City to shop in a mall, but if for some reason your inner-mall rat needs a fix, this is one of your few options.

Takashimaya

693 Fifth Avenue bet. 54th and 55th Streets
350-0100

According to the flyers handed out by Takashimaya's dapper doormen, this department store is located "On Fifth Avenue between Tokyo and Paris." Actually it's between 54th and 55th Streets, an address that you should keep on file if you're wanting unique and beautiful gifts that justify the expense.

Opened in 1993, Tak was designed to cross a futuristic Japanese aesthetic with traditional French decadence. The setting is as modern and luxuriously understated as the renovated Peninsula Hotel across the avenue: all marble floors, luxe carpets, cream-colored walls, and muted tones. On entering you're confronted with a lavish collection of flowers put together by florist Christian Tortu. Considered by many to be the top florist in town, Tortu manages to find such unusual blooms as green-colored roses. Throughout the other six floors are fancy gifts, beautiful clothing, and wonderful home furnishings, all with an elegant, often minimalist feel. This is also one of the best places in the city to find fancy pet accessories and clothing.

The fifth and sixth floors have fantastic views of Fifth Avenue. Conversely, in the windowless basement, you'll find the appropriately named Tea Box where you can sit and sip or shop for loose leaves and teapots.

While you're there...

Elizabeth Arden, 691 Fifth Avenue bet. 54th and 55th Streets, 546-0200 • A day spa and store featuring the gamut of Arden products and spa treatments. Treat yourself to a manicure in the stunning nail room, designed to resemble a Viennese ballroom.

Façonnable, 689 Fifth Avenue at 54th Street, 319-0111 • More ties than can be imagined at this specialty store which also carries a smaller range of other guy stuff—including cufflinks and other accessories.

The Museum Company, 673 Fifth Avenue at 53rd Street, 758-0976 • If you're the type who spends as much time perusing a museum's store as you do viewing the exhibits, this is the place for you. Greeting cards, gifts, and books-mostly based on the world's artistic masterpieces.

Museum of Modern Art Store, 11 West 53rd Street bet. Fifth and Sixth Avenues, 767-1050 • Postcards, books, and gifts inspired by, and relating to, the Museum's collection of 20th century art.

Chelsea and the Flatiron District

ALTHOUGH CHELSEA (14th to 30th Street, west of Sixth Avenue) is home to a slew of interesting little stores, for most shoppers the neighborhood means the big discount names on Sixth Avenue: Bed, Bath & Beyond, Old Navy, T.J. Maxx, Filene's, and Loehmann's. On weekends, Chelsea also plays host to the city's largest fleamarket, with over 500 vendors gathering to sell their wares. The locus for the Annex Flea is Sixth Avenue between 25th and 26th Streets, although there are smaller markets adjacent on 25th and 26th Street and further north along the avenue. At Chelsea's southernmost point on the far westside is where you'll find the Meatpacking District. This area is gentrifying at an amazing pace—doubtless more stores will open there soon.

IN THE FLATIRON DISTRICT (14th Street to 30th Street, Sixth Avenue to Park Avenue South) ABC Carpet and Home is the standout. This legendary store has attracted a number of pale imitators which cluster around the dramatic Flatiron Building. Lots of the major chains and the original Barnes and Noble bookstore can be found here on Lower Fifth Avenue.

Candleschtick

181 Seventh Avenue bet. 20th and 21st Streets
924-5444

Nowhere but New York would you find an entrepreneur with enough chutzpah to name his store Candleschtick. Candleschtick is Andrew Golz's very own candle superstore. Here are votives, tapers, beeswax candles, scented candles, floating candles, candles in the shape of animals, candles in terracotta pots, candles in every color of the rainbow, and even just plain candles. There are sculpted candles, candles made by artists, enormous candles with up to eight wicks and long-lasting candles that burn for hundreds of hours.

Then there's the candle paraphernalia: candelabra, wall sconces, votive holders, and miniature lampshades for your candles. Candleschtick even has candle making kits. And when you get tired of looking at candles, you can check out the store's pleasing selection of potpourri, art stamps, and greeting cards.

You'll find another location for Candleschtick at 2444 Broadway between 90th and 91st Streets, 787-5444.

While you're there...

Dish Is, 143 West 22nd Street bet. Sixth and Seventh Avenues, 352-9051 • Colorful tableware with the emphasis on bold patterns, bright colors, and chunky designs.

Bedford Downing, 156 West 22nd Street bet. Sixth and Seventh Avenues, 861-2634 • Beautiful handmade, freestanding, glass picture frames. Watch the artist at work at his in-store studio.

New York Cake and Baking, 56 West 22nd bet. Fifth and Sixth Avenues, 675-2253 • The best specialty bakeware store—everything from cake tins to icing bags and mixing bowls.

A Different Light Bookstore, 151 West 19th Street bet. Sixth and Seventh Avenues, 989-4850 • This country's biggest gay, lesbian, transsexual, and transgender mega-bookstore is your best bet for gay literature, CDs, videos, and magazines.

Albert Sakhai, 144 West 19th Street bet. Sixth and Seventh Avenues, 647-1241 • This excellent costumier creates imaginative outfits to exact specifications.

The Barneys Co-op, 236 West 18th Street bet. Seventh and Eighth Avenues, 826-8900 • Thankfully, Barneys has a downtown presence again, selling designer casualwear for men and women. The store also has accessories, cosmetics and shoes.

Dave's

581 Sixth Avenue bet. 16th and 17th Streets
800-543-8558

Whenever my two younger sisters visit from England, there's one place they always want to go for jeans and sweats. Not to the Gap, not to Old Navy, and not even to Canal Jeans. They want to go to Dave's. What could be the lure of such a nondescript place? Well, while New Yorkers, and Americans in general, are perfectly used to spending next to nothing on good quality jeans and workwear, Europeans still have to pay exorbitant prices on such standard stuff. Not only does Dave's have Levi's and Cahartt in excess, it also has them at the cheapest prices in the city.

This friendly, family-owned store, in business since 1963, continues to sell such staples as Wrangler and Lee jeans, Red Wing shoes, Cat boots, and Hanes tees at ground-scraping prices. So even if you're not visiting from Europe, Dave's should be your first port of call for cheap-as-can-be, tough-as-nails, all-American gear.

Jazz Record Center

236 West 26th Street bet. Seventh and
Eighth Avenues, 8th Floor • 675-4480

Considering this is New York City, the spiritual home of jazz, you'd expect at least a few excellent jazz record stores. Actually, the only one that really measures up is Jazz Record Center. Hidden away in a Chelsea commercial building, its collection of 45s and 78s assembled on one spacious floor span the period from the invention of mass-produced vinyl in the late 1910s to its demise in the late 1980s. Everything here is, of course, secondhand, but owner Fred Cohen only stocks albums in top condition (including lots and lots of Blue Note titles). The place seems to invite the serious aficionado and mere enthusiast in equal measure.

The records here are arranged by artist in "low-fi" cardboard cartons, and because the shop isn't challenged for space (like many New York record stores), those cartons aren't stuffed to capacity—they're half-full, so you can comfortably flip through the selections. The Center also carries an excellent selection of postcards, books, and videos, and, of course, the music you'll hear in the background is jazz, just jazz.

While you're there...

Eclectic Home, 224 Eighth Avenue bet. 21st and 22nd Streets, 255-2373 • A really good selection of home accessories to add color, invention, and cool to even the most dingy pad.

Jeffrey NY

449 West 14th Street bet. Ninth and Tenth Avenues
206-1272

effrey Kalinsky gave the Meatpacking District a much-needed shot of shopping glamor when he opened up his own department store here in 1999. Until then, this off-the-beaten track area, home to the coolest new bars and restaurants in New York, was devoid of shops. Now you'll see uptown and downtown girls alike, tripping along the western edges of the island in their Manolo's just to pay a visit to Jeffrey. This 12,000 square foot, all-white emporium, housed in a former Nabisco Foods warehouse, is the brainchild of Kalinsky, a former buyer for Barneys who founded the prototype for this store in Atlanta. Jeffrey NY is large, but not so large as to be overwhelming, and the racks here are laden with an immaculate selection of designer clothing for men and women, including Jil Sander, Michael Kors and Alexander McQueen's sought-after jeans line. But the real treat of a visit to Jeffrey is the shoe selection, which seems to spill over into every area of the store. A diverse range of designs include those by Prada, Dolce & Gabbana, Jil Sander and Manolo Blahnik as well

as lesser-known names from America and beyond. This should be your first port of call if you're looking for a perfect pair of party shoes. The accessories are equally delectable and the beauty products include those created by the New York pharmacy Bigelow's. Dotted around the store are comfy benches and seats to rest your weary feet and the dressing rooms are so spacious, you could throw a small party in them. In fact, the atmosphere here is so conducive to shopping that you may even find yourself heeding the signs splashed on every wall: WHY NOT?

While you're there...

The Ink Pad, 22 Eighth Avenue at 12th Street, 463-9876 • Every kind of rubber stamp imaginable, from stamps for the office to art stamps and stamps for kids. If you don't see what you want, you can custom order.

Commes des Garçons, 520 West 22nd Street bet. Tenth and Eleventh Avenues, 604-9200 • This incredible store, with its space-age design, is a fitting showcase for Rei Kawakubo's avant garde clothing for men and women.

Somethin' Else!, 182 Ninth Avenue bet. 21st and 22nd Streets, 924-0006 • Part antique store, part gift store, part collector's resource, Somethin' Else is New York's very own curiosity shop. Shelves are lined with every kind of collectible trinket.

Parke & Ronen, 176 Ninth Avenue bet. 20th and 21st Streets, 989-4245 • Chic urban separates for men and women by New York designers Parke Lutter and Ronen Jehezkel.

ABC Carpet & Home

888 Broadway bet. 18th and 19th Streets
473-3000 • www.abchome.com

*U*sually, you'll get the sensation once a year at holiday shopping time: You gaze around at the decorations and the lights, drink in the excitement, and just for a moment, the stress melts away, and that magical, childlike feeling comes over you, sending tingles down your spine. Well, you can get that feeling any day of the week at ABC Carpet & Home.

New York's beloved home furnishings store never fails to beguile. On entrance, you'll encounter "The Parlor," an entire floor organized as if this were the mansion of some eccentric and well-travelled Victorian millionaire. Venetian chandeliers hang next to Tiffany-style lamps, day beds drip with damasks and velvets, overstuffed chairs are filled with plump tapestry pillows, painted terracotta pots are brimming with silk flowers, an antique bird-cage keeps company with a modern mosaic table.

Upstairs and down, you'll find mammoth departments devoted to each of the following: fabrics and trimmings, the bed and bathroom, kitchenware, antiques and reproductions. Sure, there are some items at ABC that are priced beyond the average pocket, but there are infinite numbers of good deals, too, and everything here is top-notch quality. Simply put—there's nothing like it, home or abroad. Across the street is ABC's massive floorcovering department, which carries 35,000 rugs from the world over.

While you're there...
Restoration Hardware, 935 Broadway at 22nd Street,

260-9479 • The first New York location for this mini-chain selling retro-inspired home accessories and gifts, including their range of cleaning products based on old-fashioned faithfuls.

Academy Records and CDs

12 West 18th Street bet. Fifth and Sixth Avenues
242-3000 • www.academyrecords.com

Academy Books, a used-book store which formerly occupied the store next door to Academy Records, went out of business early 2000. But thankfully, the excellent adjacent used record store survives, and since its recent renovation, it's better than ever.

Most used record stores around town specialize in popular music, so Academy stands out. This is the premier place in the city to find secondhand classical and jazz copies on both CD and vinyl. Academy also has smaller sections for dance music and hip-hop. The sections are comprehensive, and the staff are knowledgeable. Prices are incredibly low and it's worth looking out for the unopened copies dotted in with the used ones-these constitute the best bargains in the store. Cassettes and DVDs are also carried and Academy will buy your high-quality, good-condition, unwanted music in any format.

While you're there...

Books of Wonder, 16 West 18th Street bet. Fifth and Sixth Avenues, 989-3270 • Simply the best children's bookstore in the city. The store has regular readings and events for kids.

Skyline Books and Records, 13 West 18th Street bet. Fifth and Sixth Avenues, 759-5463, skyline1@interport.net. • Secondhand reading and listening material of the highest quality. Book searches, too.

Paper Access, 23 West 18th Street bet. Fifth and Sixth Avenues, 463-7035 • A mammoth stationery store with a range of products both comprehensive and price-friendly.

The Fan Club

22 West 19th Street bet. Fifth and Sixth Avenues
929-3349

Every store tells a story, and none more intriguing than the one behind this glamorous clothing consignment store. The Fan Club's origins date back to the 1960s, when co-owner Gene London was the host of the popular kids' show, "The Gene London Show." The show shared a studio with the Mike Douglas program, so London got the chance to ask the stars of the time, such as Joan Crawford and Lucille Ball, for items from their wardrobes as keepsakes. Over the years, the TV host acquired one of the most comprehensive collections of sartorial memorabilia in the country.

Flash forward to 1994, when, with the help of partner John Thomas, London opened The Fan Club. This friendly place is overflowing with fabulous apparel—evening gowns cram the racks and sequined tuxes drip from the ceiling. Thanks to London's passion for charismatic clothing, many of the glittery items on offer have been requisitioned from movies, TV, and the theater. In the past, Fan Club has sold clothing which once graced the buff bodies of Madonna, Cher, and Raquel Welch (with proceeds going to benefit local charities). Thankfully, London has resisted demands to sell his enormous personal stash of celebrity castoffs. The collection remains intact, albeit in storage.

While you're there...

Darrow, 7 West 19th Street bet. Fifth and Sixth Avenues, 800-760-1552, www.darrowvintage.com • Many will cite Darrow as their favorite vintage clothing store in the city. Wonderful frocks from the 20s through the 70s and a fine selection of shoes.

Sam Flax, 12 West 20th Street bet. Fifth and Sixth Avenues, 620-3038 • A great place for very special stationery, Flax's has top-notch notebooks, journals, and photograph albums.

Fishs Eddy

889 Broadway at 19th Street • 420-9020

www.citysearch.com/nyc/fishseddy

*I*f you have kids (or if you're just plain clumsy), you should know about Fishs Eddy. The store with the distinctive checkerboard front is filled with virtually unbreakable, industrial strength china. "We've used our bowls to hammer nails into the wall," boasts one staffer. Originally, Fishs Eddy came into existence to supply hotels, restaurants and other institutions, but soon owners Julie Gaines and David Lenovitz realized that the products—designed to take daily abuse from dishwashers and klutzy servers—were just what the average home needed.

Many of the well-priced items sold here are the spoils of hotels or restaurants which have gone out of business, so they're covered with fun, funky logos. Recently, the shop introduced its own line of designs on standard china, including one that features a motif based on the Manhattan skyline (an excellent souvenir idea). Also to be found here are glasses, dishtowels, and napkins, as well as vintage tableware from the 30s, 40s, and 50s. Just make certain you truly love the items you buy—this invincible stuff will be with you for many, many years to come.

You'll find other locations for Fishs Eddy at 2176 Broadway at 77th Street, 873-8819, and 60 Mercer Street at Broome Street.

While you're there...

XYZ Total Home, 15 East 18th Street bet. Fifth Avenue and Broadway, 388-1942 • Well-priced gifts and home accessories on a smaller scale than the enormous ABC Carpet & Home (from which XYZ's name is obviously inspired).

Just Bulbs

936 Broadway bet. 21st and 22nd Streets • 228-7820

What's in a name? Everything in the case of Just Bulbs, an example of the New York specialty store taken to an extreme. The store was once the subject of a David Letterman Late Show skit in which Dave cornered a helpless staffer and asked her what she sold. "Just bulbs," replied the poor woman. "Do you sell lampshades?" "No, just bulbs."

While the idea of a store devoted entirely to Mr. Edison's invention may sound silly, Just Bulbs is actually a godsend. Every type of bulb, from halogen to high wattage, is stocked here. There's an enormous selection of string lights, which come in such ridiculous shapes as skeletons, basketballs, chili peppers, and sombreros. Nothing is overpriced, so even if you can't afford to redesign the lighting in your pad, you can at least afford to pick up a pack of apricot-colored low-wattage bulbs for adding atmosphere.

While you're there...

The Dart Shoppe, 30 East 20th Street between Broadway and Park Ave South, 533-8684 • Boards, "arrows," and free advice on how to play the British pub game.

Paragon Sporting Goods

867 Broadway bet. 17th and 18th Streets • 255-8036

*U*rban athletes have been making their way to the one-and-only Paragon since it first opened its doors in 1908-and with good reason. No matter how obscure the sport (bocce, anyone?) somewhere within Paragon's expansive three floors lurks the equipment you'll need to play it.

Paragon is like one hundred specialty sports stores rolled into one. You could shop for wetsuits, table tennis balls, ski boots, swim goggles, in-line skates, golf shoes, and frisbees and never leave the building. The store caters to fencers and weightlifters, croquet players and triathletes, water-skiers and boxers alike. You could have your old tennis racquet restrung here, or a pair of skis tuned. The store has a special sports medicine concession and a skateboard customizing service. Oh, in case you're just looking for sneakers and sweats, those are here too.

If you're looking for discounted goods, however, you should probably look elsewhere (the emphasis here is on quality and selection first and foremost). Nevertheless, Paragon is a favorite with overseas visitors-perhaps it's because there are Paragon staff members who speak a total of seven languages.

Reminiscence

50 West 23rd Street bet. Fifth and Sixth Avenues
243-2292

eminiscence—the name says it all—is a store filled with all kinds of nostalgia-inducing stuff. While Proust had his madeleines, we have our Magic 8 balls and our Mr. Potatoheads: The toys, clothing, gifts and greeting cards here are likely to provoke instant remembrance of things past. Try on a boob tube or shake your booty inside a hula hoop; give a little squeeze to the Pillsbury Doughboy or stare into the eyes of a postcard Elvis; try on a pair of Lolita heart-shaped glasses or grab a pair of fuzzy dice to hang from the rearview mirror of your Mustang. If you're too young to remember these things the first time around, Reminiscence even has books on nostalgia so you can buff up. throughout the store, you'll find a really good selection of vintage clothing and dead-stock (never-before-worn vintage duds) for men and women.

While you're there...

Medici Shoes, 24 West 23rd Street bet. Fifth and Sixth Avenues, 604-0888 • A very good resource for low-priced, fashion-inspired footwear.

La Galleria La Rue, 12 West 23rd Street bet. Fifth and Sixth Avenues, 807-1708 • Fabulously bold and colorful clothing and accessories from Europe and beyond selected with care and originality.

West Village

THE WEST VILLAGE (Houston to 14th Street, west of Fifth Avenue) still counts as Manhattan's prettiest neighborhood, despite the crowds who gather here in the summer and at weekends. Wander down streets lined with trees, brownstones, street cafes, and interesting little stores, and you'll see how the Village earned its name. Worth noting: For shoes, make for the concentration of discount shoe stores on 8th Street (between Sixth Avenue and Broadway).

Alphaville

226 West Houston bet. Sixth Avenue and
Varick Street • 675-6850

*L*et Alphaville be a lesson to you. If you hold onto your breakfast cereal giveaways long enough, they'll eventually be worth some money. Alphaville carries only mint-condition pop culture collectibles: vintage promotional products, children's toys, nostalgia, and novelties. Everything is housed in sleek glass cabinets in an all-white, gallery-like setting where a piece of gaudy merchandise can be elevated to the status of art object.

In case this sounds like the kind of place where only serious collectors can afford to shop, be assured that owners Steve Karchin and Gary Kraut opened Alphaville for the express purpose of selling to folks who just wanted a piece to dot around the apartment. For this reason they keep their prices low (often lower than the fleamarkets). Besides a huge range of goofy kids' toys from the 30s through the 70s, Alphaville specializes in vintage movie posters and advertising signs, as well as winking, 3-D flicker items-which explains why shoppers at Alphaville are often seen slowly swaying from side to side.

Aphrodisia

264 Bleecker Street bet. Sixth Avenue
and Seventh Avenue South • 989-6440

ontrary to appearances, this sparkling, new-age apothecary has been in business since 1967, and contrary to its name (a reference to the Greek goddess of love, Aphrodite), this isn't a place to buy aphrodisiacs. You will, however, run across a number of potent remedies that can be used to arouse the senses: Aphrodisia carries over 80 dried herbs and spices for both culinary and medicinal purposes

Aphrodisia has a strict "all-natural policy," so its products are as pure and unadulterated as can be. That earthy philosophy is extended to the wonderful range of bath and beauty products which include cosmetics, essential oils, fragrances, homeopathic remedies, and even home spa kits. The store has an equally impressive array of books on alternative and natural living. And, if you really are looking for an aphrodisiac, Aphrodisia does have sensual massage oils.

While you're there...

Second Childhood, 283 Bleecker Street bet. Sixth Avenue and Seventh Avenue South, 989-6140 • Antique toys and collectibles from the early part of the century through the 50s. Rocking horses are a specialty.

Bigelow Chemist

414 Sixth Avenue bet. 8th and 9th Streets
473-7324, 533-2700

Celebrity spotters take note-at Bigelow's you never know who you might run into shopping for a can of elastoplast. Liv Tyler and Kate Moss are regular customers, so if you'd like to find out how these beauties stays radiant, make a bee-line for Bigelow's.

Founded two doors down from the current location in 1838, the store retains its old-fashioned apothecary feel (and its original Victorian shop fittings). Besides a prescription counter and the usual shampoo and soap staples, Bigelow's has a superb range of imported products: hair care from France, toothpaste from Italy, manicure sets from Germany. Its sections for homeopathic and herbal remedies are especially impressive. Recently, the store started its own make-up line, called Alchemy. Appropriately, Bigelow's has taken its diverse band of customers into account when designing the line: Alchemy's myriad colors suit all skin-tones and tastes. And as befits one of the oldest stores in New York, Bigelow's staff is as helpful and friendly as can be.

While you're there...

Urban Outfitters, 374 Sixth Avenue at Waverly Place, 677-9350 • A downtown location for the hip housewares and clothing chain.

Bombalulu's

101 West 10th Street bet. Sixth and
Greenwich Avenues • 463-0897

There's something to be said for restricting your demographic to the under-six set—you end up with a store filled with lots and lots of fun items. This cheerful kids' store carries toys and clothing for little tots. The supplies here are in constant flux, but in the past I've tracked down made-in-China concertinas, plastic dino figures, mini-Super 8 viewers, reproduction tin toys, and pretty butterfly-shaped kites. The store also keeps a perennial supply of toys inspired by those icons of kiddy culture: Curious George, Madeleine, and Felix the Cat. Thankfully, there's not a Barney toy or Barbie doll in sight.

Bombalulu's stands apart from the many other excellent kids' stores in New York for one very good reason. All the kids' clothes here are manufactured especially for the store. Laundry-saving reversible jackets are a big sell, as are T-shirts and rompers printed with yellow New York taxicabs-the best baby souvenirs in the city. This is a great place to shop for dress-up gear (like frothy tutus and lizard outfits) for Halloween.

You'll find another location for Bombalulu's at 332 Columbus Avenue between 75th and 76th Streets, 501-8248.

Chelsea Garden Center

435 Hudson Street bet. Leroy and Mortaon Streets
727-7100 • www.chelseagardencenter.com

*P*ity Gotham's gardeners—in the absence of space for gardens, most of them have to make do with window boxes, roof gardens and indoor plants. Chelsea Garden Center is where those thwarted green-thumbs come to shop for supplies—everything from soil and compost to pots and, of course, the plants to put them in. There are three locations in Manhattan, and only one of them is in Chelsea. The largest, Chelsea Garden Center Home, on Hudson Street, is on the scale of a small department store. This 6,000 foot space is packed with outdoor furniture, plants, pots and garden-related gifts.

Look out for pottery from all over the world, and huge, loft-sized tropical plants, specially acclimatized for New York apartments. There's also a corner for children's clothing, garden books and tools.

For plants and pots only, make for the store's nursery, Chelsea Garden Center East, located at 321 Bowery on the corner of Second Street, 777-4500. This former parking lot is unrecognizable from its former incarnation. Here you can find trees, shrubs, perennials, annuals, seeds, and planters. The original store, the Chelsea Garden Store, located at 205 Ninth Avenue between 22nd and 23rd Streets, 741-6052, continues to supply garden furniture and meditative miniature fountains, as well as tropical plants, garden-related gifts and a wall of garden books. Friendly, expert advice is always on hand at all three locations to help you create your city garden. And if you're stuck for ideas, there's also a garden design service.

Hudson Street Papers

357 Bleecker Street bet. West 10th and
Charles Streets • 229-1064

The original Hudson Street Papers, which started life on the corner of Hudson and Bank Streets, served the neighborhood as a kind of community center and general paper-and-gift-shop combined. Now located in the heart of the West Village, the emphasis on beautiful gifts and stationery products continues.

Many-colored paper lanterns hang from the ceiling, and gorgeous journals and notebooks are dotted around on tables. Lovely and unusual gift wraps, trimmings, and greeting cards are a specialty here, making it a great place to visit at holiday time. Good quality kids' stuff includes dinky stuffed animals and picturebooks, while grownups can shop for wonderful soaps, aromatherapy oils, scented candles, and a variety of hand-selected imported items.

While you're there...

Arlene Bowman, 353 Bleecker Street bet. West 10th and Charles Streets, 645-8740 • An eclectic range of clothing for women, some handmade, as well as bags and accessories with a unique feel.

Condomania, 351 Bleecker Street bet. West 10th and Charles Streets, 691-9442 • New York's own specialty condom store has every brand, size, flavor and color of the life-saving rubber.

Susan Parrish Antiques, 390 Bleecker Street bet. West 11th and Perry Streets, 645-5020 • Beautiful vintage and antique quilts are a specialty at this homey, inviting antiques store.

Jerry Ohlinger's Movie Material Store

242 West 14th Street bet. Seventh and Eighth Avenues • 989-0869

*I*n case you were in any doubt, the cigar chomping, mustachioed man flanked by Lucille Ball, Cary Grant, Bette Davis, and James Stewart in the painting at the front of this little store is Jerry Ohlinger, proprietor and movie buff extraordinaire. Ohlinger's store supplies movie posters and photos (mostly originals), as well as celebrity shots and program books. Some of the items date back to the earliest days of cinema. Ironically, this fascinating place, down some steps and crammed with file cabinets, looks a little like the kind of noirish hole Bogart might end up visiting while on the trail of some missing starlet.

Be warned that there's only a limited number of items on display here. By flipping through giant catalogues you can get a more accurate picture of the store's complete inventory. If something piques your interest, just ask one of the counter folk to track down your selection. Be patient. They have to search through endless cabinets out back, like fevered clerks in a Fritz Lang classic.

While you're there...

Central Carpet, 81 Eighth Avenue at 14th Street, 741-3700, www.centralcarpet.com • A store with every conceivable type of floor covering. Rugs and carpets from all over the world for your downtown studio or uptown townhouse.

Paul Smith, 108 Fifth Avenue at 16th Street, 627-9770 • The British designer's only store in New York is filled with his immaculate, tailored suits and separates as well as an eccentric array of accessories and assorted vintage objects.

Mxyplyzyk

123 and 125 Greenwich Avenue at 13th Street
989-4300

*T*he store with no vowels (it's pronounced "mix-y-plisk") has plenty of intelligent, well-priced solutions for the average cramped Manhattan apartment. No, you won't be able to buy a gadget that will miraculously push back the walls or increase the height of your ceiling, but Mxyplyzyk does have a great selection of storage boxes, wall fixtures, and generally pleasing things to make day to day habitation in the Naked City just a little more bearable.

You might leave with a clever, expandable magazine rack, an elegant, wooden desk accessory, a retro-look wall clock, or a set of "dirty" soaps (with four letter words carved into them). Other good things I've seen in the past here include French toothpaste, giant Chinese incense coils, handmade silver jewelry, and well-designed coat hooks. Coffee table books, pet accessories, and greeting cards all make a perennial appearance, and there are always lots and lots of really good lamps, all at manageable prices.

While you're there...

Our Name is Mud, 59 Greenwich Avenue at Seventh Avenue, 647-7899 • A paint-your-own-pottery place with a gift store selling handmade ceramics and candles by New York artists.

Pleasure Chest, 156 Seventh Avenue South bet. Charles and Perry Streets, 242-4185, www.apleasurechest.com • The city's most elegant erotic boutique has sexual paraphernalia from all over the world, including vibrators, massage oils, undies, calendars, novelties, videos, and CD-ROMs.

Papivore, 117 Perry Street bet. Hudson Street and Greenwich Avenue, 627-6055 • Exquisite French stationery products by Marie Papier are the order of the day at this pretty boutique which also offers a custom invite service.

Three Lives & Company

154 West 10th Street at Waverly Place • 741-2069

There are many excellent small bookstores in this city, but I'd wager that if you took a poll to see which of them New Yorkers love the best, Three Lives would come out on top. Folks adore Three Lives for many reasons, not least of which is its unmistakable black-painted storefront, complete with weathered gold lettering, well-worn awning, and bright red doors. Then there's the location—on a picturesque block—which adds to the feeling that you've been transported back to the days when the Village was the city's intellectual center. Once inside, the selection of fiction, poetry, and non-fiction lining the beautiful hardwood shelves is consummate, but never overwhelming. The staff is scholarly, and there's a heady atmosphere of erudition about the place. In spite of its modest size, Three Lives hosts a number of readings by some of the world's top authors. Simply put, people love Three Lives because it's exactly the way they imagine a New York bookstore should be.

While you're there...

M.A.C., 14 Christopher Street bet. Sixth and Seventh Avenues, 243-4150 • The preferred brand of RuPaul, M.A.C.'s professional standard cosmetics come in a huge array of colors.

Oscar Wilde Bookstore, 15 Christopher Street bet. Sixth and Seventh Avenues, 255-8097 • America's very first gay and lesbian bookstore holds an excellent, if somewhat limited, selection of books by and for gays and lesbians.

Amalgamated Home, 9, 13 and 19 Christopher Street bet. Sixth and Seventh Avenues, 255-4160 • Amalgamated takes up three separate storefronts—one for furniture and lighting, one for hardware (such as handles and rails), and one for general household sundries.

Village Chess Shop

230 Thompson Street bet. West 3rd and
Bleecker Street • 475-8130

*I*t's hard to believe, but back in the 60s and 70s Greenwich Village sustained five chess stores within a few blocks of one another. Nowadays, Village Chess is one of only two remaining where you can drop by to pick up a game and a cup of coffee. Fortunately it hasn't changed much from when its doors first opened in 1972. Folks sit at cafe tables either deep in concentration or conversation while classical music plays in the background. No appointment is needed; just find yourself an opponent and start to play.

Owners George and Ruth Frohlinde have assembled an excellent selection of chess sets, boards, and boxes in cabinets to one side of the store. There are beautifully crafted pieces made from plastic, bone, marble, and metal. Take your pick from regular sets, or those shaped as Arthurian knights, Hobbit-like goblins, or folksy African figures. Beautiful boxes and boards are constructed from fine woods, and, as befits its cerebral atmosphere, the store also has a fine selection of books.

While you're there...

Stella Dallas, 218 Thompson Street bet. West 3rd and Bleecker Streets, 674-0447 • Precious and hard-to-find vintage clothing, especially from the 40s. Prices are always reasonable, and the goods are of a very high quality. Catherine Deneuve is a customer.

East Village and Lower East Side

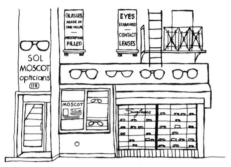

THE EAST VILLAGE (loosely defined here as 14th Street to Houston, east of Broadway) is the epicenter of downtown's explosive street culture. Here you'll find hip clothing boutiques, the best thrift shops, kitschy emporiums and trendy record stores. On St. Mark's Place (between Second and Third Avenues) street stalls sell cheap jewelry and T-shirts. Although new boutique-keepers are opening their doors on the Lower East Side (Houston to East Broadway, east of Bowery), the former stomping ground of East European immigrants hasn't changed beyond recognition. You'll still find the bargain leather goods, luggage, fabrics and housewares this neighborhood was known for; you'll just have to look harder. Try Delancey Street between Bowery and the Williamsburg Bridge, and Orchard Street between Houston and Delancey Streets.

Alphabets

115 Avenue A bet. 7th Street and St. Mark's Place
475-7250

Named for its Alphabet City location, the flagship Alphabets is really two gift stores in one, each catering to a different taste-group. The store on the left sells more refined, adult goodies such as chrome picture frames, aromatherapy candles, European soaps, and unique silver jewelry. This is the kind of stuff that would look good in an uncluttered, all-white loft with classical music on the CD player. The store on the right carries items to satisfy your inner kid (or a kid in your life) such as fun T-shirts, silly toys, kitschy nostalgia and zany greeting cards. This is the kind of stuff that would look good in a crowded and colorful studio with pop songs blaring from the radio. Whichever side of the equation suits you, Alphabets cover the bases. Be warned—in December you'll have to share the store with crowds of frazzled shoppers thanking their stars for this essential place.

You'll find other locations for Alphabets at 47 Greenwich Avenue between Perry and Charles Streets, 229-2966 and 2284 Broadway between 82nd and 83rd Streets, 579-5702.

While you're there...

Lancelotti Housewares, 66 Avenue A bet. 4th and 5th Streets, 475-6851 • This cheap and cheerful housewares store carries everything for the kitchen and home that's sleek, colorful, and well-priced.

Exit 9, 64 Avenue A bet. 4th and 5th Streets, 228-0145 •
Unusual and inventive candles, purses, essential oils, bath products, greeting cards, and some vintage items.

Anna

150 East 3rd Street bet. Avenues A and B • 358-0195

his tiny, white-painted boutique with the blue awning on the edge of the East Village was formerly devoted solely to vintage clothing. Nowadays, the store's owner, Kathy Kemp, has started designing and making her own clothes, to great success. She hasn't given up her emphasis on vintage designs however. Many of her creations are inspired by favorite vintage numbers and select items of used clothing are still slotted in amongst the new clothes on the racks.

The wonderful thing about Anna is that you never know what you might find here next. Whether you need a daytime skirt or a simple evening dress, there's always something interesting to unearth. Kemp likes to use her friends and customers for inspiration, and she has a talent for great cutting and a disregard for mere trendiness that's always refreshing. She adds new designs on an almost weekly basis, either her own, or vintage finds from regular shopping trips. And as she never makes more than a small batch of each design, you'll always have something more original than the usual chain-store fodder. In the past, Kemp's bold slip dresses with rouched fronts and brightly colored silk skirts have been big sellers, but who knows what she might create next?

While you're there...

Primal Stuff, 189 East 3rd Street bet. Avenues A and B, 674-1491 • Avant-garde, custom leather work (including corsets) by Ligea Stein, whose clients have included Cher and Aerosmith.

Dancetracks, 91 East 3rd Street between First and Second Avenues, 260-8729 • Records and CDs with a dance-music emphasis. Rare classics, imports, mix tapes and accessories.

L'Atelier, 89 East 2nd Street bet. First Avenue and Avenue A, 677-4983 • The creations of three jewelers working in striking contrast. Everything here is made to order in precious metals.

It's a Mod, Mod World, 85 First Avenue bet. 5th and 6th Streets, 460-8004, www.citysearch.com/nyc/modworld • Kitsch and pop items, and some recycled art and home furnishings. Look for the lamps made from old toasters.

Bond 07

7 Bond Street bet. Broadway and Lafayette Street
677-8487

orry, James, but the name of this pretty boutique refers to its location. Inside Bond 07, an immaculate array of accessories, cosmetics, clothing, hats, antiques, and objets all vie for attention. It's easy to imagine the great style icons of the 50s and 60s shopping happily here. Catherine Deneuve would pick out a pair of bright, modish sunglasses, Audrey Hepburn would opt for a handmade cocktail hat, and Julie Christie would leave with rosewater facial tonic from London.

This isn't the only store presided over by energetic

owner Selima Salaun-she's also the force behind Selima Optique, an eyewear boutique, and Le Corset, a lingerie store. Bond 07 is filled with a combination of items that show off Salaun's exacting good taste, including, of course, specs and undies. As with many of the boutiques in Noho and Little Italy, prices at Bond 07 aren't for those on a budget, but the store's carefully chosen contents are as irresistible to women as, well, 007 himself.

While you're there...

The Art Store, 1-5 Bond Street bet. Broadway and Lafayette Streets, 533-2444 • Opened in 1997, this store is a welcome addition to downtown's art scene. Paints, paper, brushes, and every imaginable art supply in a spacious setting.

Daryl K, 21 Bond Street at Lafayette, 777-0713 • Downtown designer Daryl Kerrigan is endlessly imitated by the folks on Seventh Avenue. Try on a pair of DK's signature hipster pants-they fit like a dream.

Katayone Adeli, 35 Bond Street bet. Lafayette Street and Bowery, 260-3500 • Adeli's perfect pants have won her a cult following that includes Gwyneth Paltrow. Delectable cashmere sweaters and dresses too.

Footlight Records

113 East 12th Street bet. Fourth Avenue and
Broadway • 533-1572 • www. footlight.com

*T*here are those who can't resist a good show tune, and then there are those who would rather suffer the tortures of the damned than listen to the soundtrack to *Sweet Charity*. Thanks to my grandfather, who taught me all the songs from the musicals, I fall into the former camp. Anyone else who feels the same way should check out Footlight Records, the Great White Way of record stores. If you're looking for show tunes and cast recordings, Footlight has it all. Ask a staffer for the cast recording of *Phantom of the Opera*, and he'll ask you if you want the New York, Japanese, German, or Swedish version.

Footlight doesn't stop at musicals—you'll also find a huge selection of movie soundtracks, jazz recordings, cabaret cuts, and big band numbers. There's a 50% split between vinyl and CDs-the vinyl is mainly used, while the CDs are mainly new. Movie studios, ad agencies, and fashion designers have come to rely on Footlight to provide them with music for films, commercials, and runway shows. And if the names Frank, Judy, Bing, and Shirley make you weak at the knees, you might come to rely on Footlight, too.

H

*T*his particular block of 9th Street is packed with great stores—in fact, this is one of the best shopping blocks in the East Village—but H stands out from the crowd. A kind of Takashimaya in miniature, minus the clothing and exorbitant prices, H is brimful with interesting gifts and home accessories.

In the past I've found clever gadgets (such as a flower stand that keeps fresh flowers alive longer), beautiful ornaments (a glass paperweight with a dandelion clock inside), and uniquely useful items (crystal beaded pouches to hang over light bulbs, giving off a gentle, speckled light). Everything has a creative, unusual, one-of-a-kind feel.

Besides seeking out items for the store, owner Craig Higgins makes the lamps you'll find here. Taking his inspiration wherever he finds it, he constructs exquisite creations from Rolls Royce engine parts, cut glass decanters, old milk glass, construction workers' lamps, and crab pots. And, like everything else at H, they're beautiful, functional, and unlike anything you've ever seen.

While you're there...

Jutta Neuman, 317 East 9th Street bet. First Avenue and Avenue A, 982-7048 • Handmade leather bags and shoes by this German shoemaker. Neuman's footwear is a favorite with practically every designer on Seventh Avenue.

Cobblestones, 314 East 9th Street bet. First Avenue and Avenue A, 673-5372 • The grandmother's attic of your dreams. Cobblestones has irresistible vintage hats, gloves, shoes, scarves, housewares and trinkets.

Transitions, 309 East 9th Street bet. First Avenue and Avenue A, 254-9188 • Original handmade lamps and steel furniture by Walter Watson. His wife Nicole fills the back part of the store with luxe antique and vintage clothing. The pair also offers an excellent interior design service.

Manhattan Portage, 333 East 9th Street bet. First and Second Avenues, 594-7068 • The flagship store for this brand's popular, utilitarian, hard-wearing bags and backpacks.

Kiehl's

109 Third Avenue between 13th and 14th Streets
677-3171

*A*sk any Hollywood celebrity for a list of favorite beauty products, and you can bet they mention Kiehl's. The cult brand, which shuns artificial ingredients and fancy packaging, attracts such famous (and famously fussy) clients as Demi Moore and Sharon Stone, proving once and for all that a good product will sell, even without an expensive advertising campaign.

Nowadays, Kiehl's carries a full range of balms, salves, moisturizers, skin creams, (in fact any product you might use on the body), but the brand started life in the early part of the century just one door down from its current location. This was a pharmacy, whose founder, John Kiehl, would cook up skin creams and other facial tonics in the back room. Kiehl's products managed to stand the test of time, although the same can't be said of Kiehl himself, who sold the store to the Morse family in the 1920s. A Morse descendent, Jami Heidegger, heads up this genuinely old-fashioned place which has retained the wall fixtures from the original pharmacy, as well as the Morse family's amazing collection of antique motorcycles (go figure). Best of all, the staff is attentive and courteous (in spite of the crowds lured here by Kiehl's excellent reputation worldwide). In this age of quick-fix consumerism, that's no mean feat.

While you're there...

Air Market, 97 Third Avenue bet. 12th and 13th Streets, 995-5888, www.airmarket.com • Japanese imports, kooky clothing, and a ton of Hello Kitty trinkets.

Apartment 141, 141 East 13th Street bet. Fourth Avenue and Broadway, 982-4227 • Colorful vintage clothing in an apartment-like setting. Some new stuff is thrown into the mix.

Metropolis, 43 Third Avenue bet. 9th and 10th Streets, 358-0795 • A sister store to the Metropolis on Avenue B between 6th and 7th Streets. Lots of good quality vintage and new streetwear in an East Village vein.

99X, 84 East 10th Street bet. Third and Fourth Avenues, 460-8599 • A great selection of Doc Marten shoes and other modish British imports such as Ben Sherman shirts and classic bomber jackets.

Other Music

15 East 4th Street bet. Broadway and
Lafayette Streets • 477-8150

Why Other Music? The name makes sense once you take into account this record store's location: across the street from Tower Records. Other Music is exactly that—a resource for hard-to-find imports, obscure recordings, and the latest sounds from Europe—specialties you'd be lucky to find anywhere in the city, let alone at the aforementioned megastore.

Other Music could fit into Tower Records fifty times over, but this tiny store beats the giant hands down for musical variety and peculiarity. Movie soundtracks, French pop from the 60s, techno, ambient, drum and bass, and whatever else is now are all in plentiful supply. The racks here are picked over by some of the most musically correct folks in the city, but there's plenty of fodder for the amateur ear-whimsical novelties like *The Best of Brigitte Bardot*, or kitschy cocktail music compilations. When a friend fell in love with the music to a Werner Herzog's film Aguirre, this is where she found the CD-and 10 others by the same composer.

While you're there...

Naked Ape, 36 East 4th Street bet. Bowery and Lafayette Street, 254-9011 • This British-owned shop has a good range of young and affordable women's clothing and accessories—everything that's fun to put on.

Dollhouse, 400 Lafayette Street at 4th Street, 308-0055 • The flagship store for the junior label. Mostly kooky and occasionally sophisticated girlswear.

Screaming Mimi, 382 Lafayette Street bet. 4th and Great Jones Streets, 677-6464 • Vintage and new clothing, as well as housewares, at this internationally known New York store.

Shakespeare & Co., 716 Broadway bet. 4th Street and Astor Place, 529-1330 • One of the best loved little bookstores in New York has all the latest titles. British imports a specialty.

Quilted Corner

120 Fourth Avenue at 12th Street • 505-6568

Sisters Susan Horovitz and Michelle Roth preside over a store so cozy, you want to hunker down and take a nap. At Quilted Corner the pair has brought together a comfy collection of antique and vintage bedding, as well as heaps of textiles dating from the 30s through the 60s. Vintage lingerie and clothing can also be found here in plentiful supply, but it's the quilts which are the main event.

If, like me, you didn't inherit a traditional American quilt, then Quilted Corner can furnish you with your very own heirloom. The pieces here are all in wonderful condition, and each item has gently faded to beautiful shades of pale. If you have a hankering to make your own quilt, the shop has stacks of vintage textiles suitable for the job. The sisters also have a great collection of tablecloths, handkerchiefs, scarves, napkins, and baby quilts, and offer a repair service as well. If it's true, as they say, that every quilt tells a story, then there's enough material at Quilted Corner for an epic novel.

While you're there...

Alabaster Bookstore, 122 Fourth Avenue bet. 12th and 13th Streets, 982-3550 • A user-friendly, and just plain friendly, used bookstore on a smaller scale than the nearby Strand.

FarFetched, 110 Fourth Avenue bet. 11th and 12th Streets, 460-8873 • Gifts, greeting cards, picture frames, and jewelry as well as toys and clothing for kids. A great selection.

Adventure Shop, 104 Fourth Avenue bet. 11th and 12th Streets, 673-4546 • Costumes aplenty, for Halloween and more. Specialists in vampire paraphernalia.

Resurrection

123 East Seventh Street bet. First Avenue and
Avenue A • 228-0063

For those who know the difference between antique Pucci and vintage Gucci, there's Resurrection. Housed in a former funeral parlor, this fabulous clothing store, with striking scarlet-colored walls, is more than a place to shop, it's a veritable fashion museum. The high-quality collection includes beaded dresses and lacy nightgowns from the early part of the century. Then there are the perfectly preserved designer frocks from the 20s through the 40s by such notable names as Courrèges and Yves St. Laurent, glitzy pantsuits made by Nudie (the man who created Elvis's stage costumes for Las Vegas), op art shifts from the 60s, and even *Dynasty* dresses from the 80s.

Budding rock stars have been known to stop by and snap up outlandish pieces, while stylists and costume designers rely on the store for inspiration and to fill in the wardrobe gaps on photo shoots. While much of the stunning array of clothing is collectible—with prices that reflect their pedigree—there are also plenty of affordable pieces thrown into the mix.

You'll find another location for Resurrection at 217 Mott Street between Prince and Spring Streets, 625-1374.

While you're there...

No XS, 80 East 7th Street bet. First and Second Avenues, 674-6753 • Deluxe hand-knits in natural yarns. A made-to-order service is available.

Fab 208, 77 East 7th Street bet. First and Second Avenues, 673-7581 • New and used clothing and accessories in a distinctive, East Village, funky fashion.

Tokio 7, 64 East 7th Street bet. First and Second Avenues, 353-8443 • This consignment store will sell your closet overflow. Lots of labels such as Gaultier, Versace, Karan, and Klein.

Enelra, 48 1/2 East 7th Street bet. First and Second Avenues, 473-2454 • Excellent lingerie store which covers the bases—everything from sexy to girlish.

Savoia

125 East 7th Street bet. First Avenue and
Avenue A • 358-9182

Frank Sinatra, Cary Grant, Jimmy Stewart. Now those were guys who knew how to dress. Tailor Michele Savoia makes clothing fit for a 40s movie god. "The look hasn't dated," says the man himself, dressed to the hilt in a baggy suit with high-waisted pants, and a pocket watch chain dangling from his vest pocket. "It's the classic American look."

Step inside Savoia's store-salon and that classic look is given its due. The space itself is reminiscent of a gentlemen's outfitter of 50 years ago with its low lighting, lush carpeted floor, and dark wood-paneled walls. Beautifully made suits in the finest wools and tweeds are available to order, or off-the-rack. (Prices, while not "cheap," are surprisingly reasonable considering the amount of hand craftsmanship involved.) You can top off your immaculate three-piece with the appropriate accessories: an antique pair of cufflinks, a felt fedora, or that essentially un-PC item, a cigarette case. Don't worry: Frank, Cary, and Jimmy would no doubt have approved.

While you're there...

Sears and Robot, 120 East 7th Street bet. First Avenue and Avenue A, 253-8719 • Japanese imports abound at this wittily named store selling anime toys, gadgets, candy, and robots (not Roebuck's).

Tompkins Square Books and Records, 111 East 7th Street bet. First Avenue and Avenue A, 979-8958 • You can rifle through piles of used books (as well as records) and then recline in a cozy chair to peruse your choice before you buy.

Body Worship, 102 East 7th Street bet. First Avenue and Avenue A, 614-0124, www.bodyworship.com • One of the best places in the city to buy latex and fetish gear. The store has outfitted everyone from Janet Jackson to the Material Girl herself.

Kimono House, 93 East 7th Street bet. First Avenue and Avenue A, 505-0232 • Gorgeous kimonos (new, vintage, and antique), as well as bags and vests made from the obi (the traditional Japanese cummerbund).

Strand Bookstore

828 Broadway at 12th Street • 473-1452

True bibliophiles and mere bargain-seekers alike adore Strand Bookstore. Established in 1927, the Strand claims to be the world's largest used bookstore. "8 miles of books" says the sign outside, which means that the store's three floors hold enough printed matter to stretch from Broadway to the New Jersey shore and back again.

The main lure, of course, is the enormous and musty selection of secondhand tomes, crammed into endless shelves on the store's first floor. Rainy afternoons pass effortlessly as you pore over dog-eared Dickens and faded Faulkners. Antique and rare books are also here in abundance.

For those who prefer their tomes pristine, however, there's also the store's basement, which houses nearly-new reviewers' copies. Here you'll find the exact same recently-released titles as at nearby Barnes & Noble, only at a third less the price. Upstairs, on the main floor, discounted publishers' overstock is piled high on tables, offering further opportunity for bargains. You'll find another location for Strand Bookstore at 95 Fulton Street between William and Gold Streets, 732-6070.

While you're there...

Forbidden Planet, 840 Broadway at 13th Street, 473-1576. • A huge selection of comics, sci fi books and related toys for kids and collectors.

Sol Moscot Opticians

118 Orchard Street at Delancey Street • 477-3796

*I*t takes tenacity to survive in retail over the duration of almost a century, so the Moscot family must have fortitude to spare. Founding father Hyman peddled eyeglasses from his pushcart on the Lower East Side in the 1900s. By 1915, Hyman's son Sol had raised funds to open a store on Rivington Street, where he stayed until moving to larger premises on nearby Orchard Street in 1941.

Sol's grandsons Harvey and Ken still preside over the Orchard Street shop with its bright yellow storefront, which only the truly myopic could miss. Inside, the only concessions to Moscot's illustrious history are the vintage optician signs in the stairwell. This is a fully modernized optometrist's office, and one of the best places in the city to find discounted eyewear. The staff is wonderfully efficient and helpful, steering you toward cheaper no-name versions of the designer frames that are also found here in plentiful supply. And if you're in a rush, not to worry, prescriptions can be made up in just an hour.

You'll find another Moscot location at 69 West 14th Street at Sixth Avenue, 647-1550.

While you're there...

Orchard Street Sunday Market, Orchard Street bet. Delancey and Houston Streets • Clothing, toys, and leather goods at bargain prices every Sunday.

Beckenstein Men's Fabrics, 133 Orchard Street bet. Delancey and Rivington Streets, 475-6666 • Quality men's suiting. Customers include top tailors, costumiers, and movie stars such as Robert De Niro.

Barsouv, 91 Orchard Street at Broome Street, 925-3400 • Lush designer fabrics, culled from the world over, in rich colors and textures for upholstery and drapes.

Lower East Side Tenement Museum Shop, 90 Orchard Street at Broome Street, 431-0233, www.wnet.org/tenement • Fascinating merchandise related to neighborhood history, including maps, postcards, books, and toys.

TG-170

170 Ludlow Street between Houston and
Stanton Streets • 995-8660 • www.tg170.com

*T*G stands for owner Terry Gillis, who started out in business on Ludlow Street selling her own T-shirts and baseball caps in 1993. When young designers came in and asked her to sell their clothing, Gillis couldn't resist, and TG-170 quickly emerged as the store for new downtown designers to showcase their stuff.

Gillis was among the first to recognize the talents of Rebecca Danenberg, Pixie Yates, and Built by Wendy, who've gone on to acquire seminal status. She continues to add new names to her line-up, including Rubin and Chapelle, whose well-made separates are slated to be the next big thing. Gillis recently introduced her own line of sleek and sassy womenswear called, appropriately enough, TG-170. Great bags and accessories are also here. And should you try on a perfect bias-cut slip dress that you just saw that impossibly waify model eyeing, you will have arrived downtown.

While you're there...

Amy Downs, 103 Stanton Street at Ludlow Street, 598-4189 • Colorful, original, and occasionally crazy handmade hats by one of downtown's favorite milliners.

Nova USA, 100 Stanton Street at Ludlow Street, 228-6944 • Basic separates for men mainly and women too that are functional but always fashionable.

Mary Adams, 159 Ludlow Street bet. Stanton and Rivington Streets, 473-0237 • Frilly, custom-made party frocks and wedding dresses in diaphanous fabrics. Entirely girlish.

Timtoum

179 Orchard Street bet. Houston and
Stanton Streets • 780-0456 • www.codek.com

"A One Stop Cosmic Shop" is how owners Erika Lively and Sasha Crnobrnja describe their mixed-up store. Timtoum is home to clothing (new and used), accessories, and records, all brought together in an old Orchard Street storefront. This place is so friendly and relaxed you'll feel happy enough to dance along to the music as you try on for size.

Crnobrnja designs the new apparel, while Lively, who used to work the fleamarket circuit, scours the state for good vintage garb. She has a great eye and never overprices. The vintage offerings are complimented by Crnobrnja's own line of sleek streetwear, called Go Global. Timtoum also carries cotton T-shirts emblazoned with designs by Claudia Pearson (who illustrated this book).

Then there's the wildly diverse record collection, including everything from world music to disco, jazz, and easy listening. Throw into the equation the occasional cowboy hat from Mexico, cotton tops made in India, and beaded purses from Nepal, and you definitely have a one-stop shop, cosmic or otherwise.

While you're there...

Cherry, 185 Orchard Street bet. Houston and Stanton Streets, 358-7131 • Colorful, collectible, vintage and antique clothing, as well as furniture and accessories, with a mod slant.

Marcoart, 186 Orchard Street bet. Houston and Stanton Streets, 253-1070, www.marcoart.com • Fun T-shirts, clothing, and bags by the irrepressible Marco (who will screen-print anything that sits still long enough).

Xuly Bët, 189 Orchard Street bet. Houston and Stanton Streets, 982-5437 • Utterly original dresses and separates by the French pioneer of deconstruction clothing design.

Juan Anon, 193 Orchard Street bet. Houston and Stanton Streets, 529-7795 • Elegant, handmade shirts in fast-forward fabrics. Custom orders are taken.

Tink

42 Rivington Street bet. Eldridge and
Chrystie Streets • 529-6356

When illustrator Claudia Pearson, whose pictures appear in this book, returned from her around the world trip in 1999 she brought back more than the usual quota of tourist souvenirs. She also brought with her an address book packed with the names of artists and artisans she had met on her travels. Pearson set to work transforming her studio on the Lower East Side into Tink, a store that serves as a colorful showcase for unique designs, art and artifacts culled from around the world.

Pearson has an excellent artist's eye. Striped bowls from South Africa are made from woven telephone wires, the brightly colored printed fabrics are from Polynesia, the beaded bracelets and bags are from Bali. Intricate sculptures made from wire and tin were found in South Africa. The walls of the space are hung with collectible hand-painted shop signs also from South Africa as well as Pearson's own paintings. Look out for the recycled radios, constructed from wire and tin cans-yes, they really do work. But not everything at Tink is from far off climes. Pearson also sells bags and jewelry by local artists, some who live as nearby as the very exotic East Village, as well as vintage ceramics found at flea markets.

While you're there...

Vinnie's Tampon Case, 245 Eldridge Street bet. Houston and Stanton Streets, 228-2273 • There's no other store like it in NYC, or anywhere else for that matter. Artist, feminist and good guy Vinnie Angel makes screenprinted cases for tampons and fridge magnets emblazoned with feminist slogans.

Soho

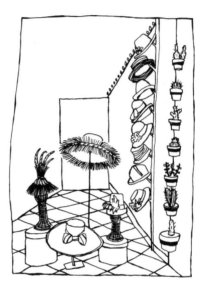

FORMERLY THE EXCLUSIVE DOMAIN OF ART GALLERIES and unique specialty stores, Soho (Houston to Canal Streets, west of Broadway) has emerged as New York's top destination for designer and nationally-known boutiques. However, there are still plenty of interesting little places to shop in the city's snazziest shopping district (and you can always gawk at the models who frequent the neighborhood). Along Broadway in addition to big name stores such as Old Navy and Banana Republic, you'll find excellent prices on sneakers at a number of cut-price sportswear stores (which actually extend as far north as 8th Street).

Broadway Panhandler

477 Broome Street bet. Greene and
Wooster Streets • 966-3434

For the most part, Soho's stunning iron-front buildings are home to chic stores selling the occasional piece of over-priced, scanty clothing in a monochrome, minimalist setting. Not at Broadway Panhandler. The best kitchen supply store in town makes the most of its lofty Soho space, cramming every square inch with pots, pans, kettles, and skillets. Prices here are often as much as 40% below retail, and Panhandler doesn't scrimp on quality—it's filled with the kind of top-notch utensils that keep professional and amateur cooks equally happy.

In business since 1976, Panhandler carries big name brands like Le Creuset, All-Clad, Calphalon, and Weber. You'll find small kitchen appliances such as blenders and electric kettles, and party novelties such as cake decorations and cocktail umbrellas. Everything for the kitchen is right here, from knives and pepper grinders to aprons and dishcloths. Add to the mix an excellent range of cookbooks, and you have a concoction which might just inspire reluctant chefs to skip the pizza delivery and handle a pan.

While you're there...

Catherine, 468 Broome Street at Greene Street, 925-6765 • French stylist and designer Catherine Maladrino's store is an homage to 60s chic. Her clothing for women features incredible detailing, but she's best know for her felt fedoras in lush colors.

Jonathan Adler, 465 Broome Street bet. Greene and Mercer Streets, 941-8950 • The place to find the complete range of home accessories by this popular designer. His op-art inspired pottery and pillows in subtle browns, blues and reds are instant design classics.

Enchanted Forest

85 Mercer Street bet. Spring and Broome Streets
925-6677 • www.citysearch.com/nyc/enchantedforest

*T*he fairy-tale name isn't superfluous—Enchanted Forest is truly one of the most magical places to shop in the city. The store, for children and their adult companions, has leafy tree branches bowing down from above and a slatted-wooden staircase leading to a little humpbacked bridge overhead. To a small child, this is a very adventurous and exciting place—well, okay, I feel that way, too.

Downstairs, the front part of the store is devoted to the tiny trinkets which kids find irresistible—little erasers, plastic critters, colored marbles, and assorted baubles. At the back, in glass cases, are more elaborate toys—many of them handmade— as well as classic children's volumes such as Peter Rabbit and Winnie the Pooh. Upstairs on the wooden mezzanine, you'll find enough soft animal toys to fill a second Ark.

Enchanted Forest's business card gushes about "celebrating the spirit of the animals, the old stories and the child within." Cynicism aside, be warned that you may get the overwhelming urge to toddle up those wooden stairs, take an oversized, fluffy frog in your arms and drool.

While you're there...

Kate Spade, 454 Broome Street at Mercer Street, 274-1991 • Good quality, fashion-worthy tote bags in black, neutrals, and bright colors of the season. Spade is much lauded for her imaginative designs.

M.A.C., 113 Spring Street bet. Mercer and Greene Streets, 334-4641 • A Soho location for the professional make-up brand, and the preferred war-paint of RuPaul.

Fragments

107 Greene Street bet. Prince and Spring Streets
334-9588

Simply put, Fragments has great jewelry. Longtime buyers Janet Goldman and Jimmy Moore supply the big department stores such as Saks, Nieman Marcus, and Barneys. Over the years they've assembled an exclusive stable of 25 or so jewelry designers who have the luxury of trying out new designs on a devoted audience at this pretty Soho store, while Goldman and Moore determine which ones will be the next big sellers for the department stores.

The result is a place where the customer rules. If it doesn't please, it doesn't last long. Although there's an enormous range of designs sold here, they have a few things in common—they are executed on a human scale, never too trendy or ostentatious, and always with an unusual or special detail or edge. While prices are not cheap, they're not out of the price range of someone looking for something both unique and extra special.

While you're there...

Zona, 97 Greene Street bet. Prince and Spring Streets, 925-6750 • Filled with good things from around the world including home accessories, some furniture, beautiful jewelry, beauty products, and lots more arranged artfully according to color and contrast.

Vivienne Tam, 99 Greene Street bet. Prince and Spring Streets, 966-2398 • Contemporary, Asian-influenced women's clothing by the designer whose cocktail dresses are on every party girl's wish list.

Face Stockholm, 110 Prince Street at Greene Street, 334-3900 • Professional-caliber make-up in an enormous palette of colors. Excellent bath and beauty products, too.

Metropolitan Museum of Art Store, 113 Prince Street bet. Greene and Wooster Streets, 614-3000 • The Met's exclusive range of reproduction jewelry and artworks as well as other trinkets inspired by its collection.

Agnès B, 116-118 Prince bet. Greene and Wooster Streets, 925-4649 • The French designer's womenwear store is just as you'd imagine it—monochromatic and filled with her immaculate, gamine designs.

Grass Roots Garden

131 Spring Street bet. Greene and Wooster Streets
226-2662

*I*f the only space you have for gardening is indoors, get yourself to the indoor Eden at Grass Roots Garden. The store has no outdoor space, so the selection here tends toward exotic plants that grow well indoors. That doesn't mean they'll need high humidity—every Grass Roots plant has been acclimatized for the Northeast and raised in shaded greenhouses so your potted item won't wilt as soon as it's placed in an apartment. All plants are sold in beautiful and roomy pots, so the usual need for repotting doesn't apply. The store also offers an excellent urban landscaping service.

Downstairs is a general store where avid gardeners and gift givers can hunt through a great range of gardening tools, seeds, books, and lots and lots of birdhouses (some of them look so inviting, you almost feel like shrinking, Alice-style, so you can climb inside). Grass Roots even has just the right kind of floppy straw gardener's hat for popping on your head while you tend to those window boxes.

While you're there...

Spring Street Market, Spring Street at Wooster Street • Just about the only place to find bargain clothing in Soho, this outdoor market has cheap, cheerful clothing and accessories.

Aero, 132 Spring bet. Greene and Wooster Streets, 966-1500 • This interior design company sells aesthetically pleasing, contemporary home furnishings and gifts.

Kirna Zabete, 96 Greene Street bet. Prince and Spring Streets, 941-9656 • This oh-so-fashionable boutique is filled with hot and hard-to-find items. Over 60 designers are represented as well as a mouthwatering array of accessories including shoes and lingerie.

Louis Vuitton, 116 Greene Street bet. Prince and Spring Streets, 274-9090 • Designer Marc Jacob's take on LV's classic designs has introduced a new generation to the concept of fine luggage.

Agnès B Homme, 79 Greene Street bet. Spring and Broome Streets, 431-4339 • An entirely elegant menswear line by the très française designer whose mod clothing was used in the film Pulp Fiction.

Helmut Lang, 80 Greene bet. Spring and Broome Streets, 925-7214 • Lang's first U.S. store is as forward-thinking as his envelope-pushing designs. Suits, separates and a jeans line for men and women.

The Hat Shop

120 Thompson Street bet. Prince and
Spring Streets • 219-1445

Effusive owner Linda Pagan prides herself on championing excellent up and coming milliners and introducing their designs at the store. Although small, the pretty blue-painted space with the feel of a 50s salon offers shoppers plenty of choice. You'll find hats for every occasion (arranged according to season) perched on hat stands and hooked onto the wall—lavish confections for dress-up events, floppy straw hats for lounging in the garden, and woolly deer-stalkers for the winter months. You might discover a towering hat made in Brooklyn designed to accommodate rasta dreads, or a frothy cocktail concoction made in South Carolina, covered all over in flowers and feathers.

Although some of her pieces are a little too outré for everyday wear (Pagan calls them her "editorial" hats), you'll also find hats that are eminently wearable and affordable. And as every hat in the store gets named after a movie star, you're bound to be entertained while you try on the "Audrey Hepburn" or the "Elizabeth Taylor."

While you're there...

Thompson Chemists, 137 Thompson Street bet. Houston and Prince Streets, 598-9790 • A pharmacy that's kept well-supplied with European remedies and beauty products. The knowledgeable staff could even save you a trip to the doctor.

Peter Fox, 105 Thompson Street, bet. Prince and Spring Streets, 431-7426 • New York's premier bridal shoe store. A large selection of styles and colors, as well generic evening shoes.

INA, 101 Thompson bet. Prince and Spring Streets, 941-4757 • A Soho location for the designer resale store. Last season's labels at manageable prices.

Hotel Venus

382 West Broadway bet. Spring and
Broome Streets • 966-4066

There are no rooms at the Hotel Venus-just a whole lot of clothing designed to make a big impression on entrance. Store impresario Patricia Fields opened her first self-titled boutique on 8th Street (10 East 8th Street between University and Fifth Avenue, 254-1699), providing drag queens, club kids, and exhibitionists with fabulous clothing in outrageous colors and larger-than-life sizes. Hotel Venus is her newer, bigger and altogether more glamorous venture (as if that were possible), and it's filled with even more rhinestone-studded, feather-covered, sequin-smattered clothing.

Housed in the same majestic, blue-painted building as the hip housewares store Dom, Hotel Venus doubles as a hair-salon specializing in, you guessed it, big hair. This is also one of the best places in the city to buy an over-the-top wig, or a pair of back-breaking high-heels. You'll also find sexy lingerie and make-up concessions, as well as lots and lots of imported Japanese sneakers, clothing, bags, and assorted rinky-dink items. And if spandex just ain't your thing, you can also get yourself immortalized on a set of stickers at the store's in-house photo-machine.

While you're there...

Dom, 382 West Broadway bet. Spring and Broome Streets, 334-5580 • Well-designed, always kooky, housewares and gifts that you won't find at Pottery Barn.

Anthropologie, 375 West Broadway bet. Spring and Broome Streets, 343-7070 • This mini-chain, with a clutch of stores across the country, is a kind of upscale Urban Outfitters. Clothing for women that's nicely luxe as well as home accessories and some furniture in a cavernous setting.

Origins, 402 West Broadway at Spring Street, 219-9764 • Excellent, all-natural, ecologically sound, untested on animals beauty products at the brand's flagship.

Polo Sport, 379 West Broadway bet. Spring and Broome Streets, 625-1660 • A downtown location for all-American designer Ralph Lauren's cheaper, younger line.

Oliver Peoples, 366 West Broadway at Broome Street, 925-5400 • The British designer's eyewear manages to be timeless and modern both. His sunglasses and frames are gaining fans worldwide.

What Goes Around Comes Around, 351 West Broadway bet. Grand and Broome Streets, 343-9303 • The best vintage clothing store in Soho has a large selection of high quality, well-priced garb, including an excellent supply of vintage and antique denim.

Kate's Paperie

561 Broadway at Prince Street • 941-9816

*I*n this age of personal computers and e-mail, the humble act of handwriting a letter or invitation is in danger of becoming a lost art. However, for those who still prefer to put pen to paper, Kate's Paperie will be heaven, and for those who get writer's cramp just thinking about picking up a pen, Kate's just might be an inspiration.

First and foremost, Kate's is a resource for beautiful, unusual, and sometimes expensive papers. Designers and artists love to frequent Kate's for its comprehensive range: over 5,000 papers in every color, texture, weight, material, and design are hung on racks all around the store. There are papers from 30 different countries; many are handmade, recycled, or both. Even if you couldn't bring yourself to scribble on such exquisite stuff, you could at least use it to wrap a very special gift. This is also a place to find wonderful fountain pens and inks (should you decide to make your mark), as well as the city's best supply of journals, date books and assorted stationery (including a complete line of Crane's). That's not to mention trimmings for wrapping gifts, paper lanterns, art stamps, greeting cards, napkins, books, bookmarks, letter openers, and paper-weights, making this place a really good bet around holiday time.

You'll find other locations for Kate's Paperie at 8 West 13th Street bet. Fifth and Sixth Avenues, 633-0570, and 1288 Third Avenue at 73rd Street, 396-3670.

While you're there...

Zara International, 580 Broadway at Prince Street, 343-1725 • A downtown location for this Spanish chain that specializes in very wearable separates for women at work and play. Your best bet if you need something cheap and cheerful, fast.

Guggenheim Museum Store, 575 Broadway at Prince Street, 423-3500 • Merchandise relating to the Museum's current shows and permanent collections, as well as interesting jewelry, books, postcards, gadgets and gifts. Also good for holiday shopping.

Sephora, 555 Broadway bet. Prince and Spring Streets, 625-1309 • The cosmetics megastore is the biggest of its kind in the world. Every shade of make-up, every kind of scent and every type of skin cream available. All the major (and some minor) cosmetic companies are represented.

Club Monaco, 520 Broadway at Spring Street, 941-1511 • One of five locations for this Canadian chain around town. For those of us who want expensive designer separates for every day but can't afford them.

Victoria's Secret, 565 Broadway bet. Prince and Spring Streets, 274-9519 • See the lingerie from the famous catalog in three dimensions, if not the supermodels, at this downtown location for the ubiquitous undies chain.

Scoop, 532 Broadway at Spring Street, 925-288 • The original downtown location for Stefani Greenfield's consummate collection of desirable clothing by New York's best small-name designers.

Canal Jeans, 504 Broadway bet. Spring and Broome Streets, 226-1130 • Something of a horror thanks to the hordes who flock here, Canal Jeans should be braved by anyone in need of a huge range of cheap denim, both new and used.

Le Corset

80 Thompson Street bet. Broome and Spring Streets • 334-4936

Women who are ready to ditch those ubiquitous sports undies, or want to make a break from the enigmatic Ms. Victoria have a problem. New York, the city with one of everything, doesn't have a single lingerie store that bears comparison to the selection of sweet nothings you'll find in Paris, Milan, or London.

Le Corset is as close as you get without hopping a flight. Besides being the best little lingerie place in town, this is also the only lingerie store to combine new designs with vintage and antique pieces. French designers such as Sybaris and Fifi Chachnil hang on racks alongside Victorian nightgowns and floaty 40s negligees. Hand-made, high priced romantic bustiers cozy up with Vivienne Westwood corsets and softest silk camisoles. The store even has its own line of colorful, net undies decorated with ribbon roses and designed by Helene Birbinkblit. Most of the slips and corsets here can double as outerwear, so you might just come away with an alternative to your ordinary undies and a new party outfit too.

While you're there...

Il Bisonte, 72 Thompson Street bet. Spring and Broome Streets, 966-8773 • A downtown location for the heavy-duty Italian leather purses and bags company.

The 1909 Company, 63 Thompson Street bet. Spring and Broome Streets, 343-1658 • A stunning collection of antique, vintage and highly collectible clothing. Bargain racks outside.

Aveda Institute, 233 Spring Street bet. Varick Street and Sixth Avenue, 807-1492 • The salon and spa also has a complete range of wholesome Aveda beauty products including purest essential oils.

Otto Tootsi Plohound

413 West Broadway bet. Prince and Spring Streets
925-8931

You can wear out your shoe leather visiting every decent shoe store in town, or alternatively, you can make one trip to Otto Tootsi Plohound, which has the city's best selection of mid-to-high priced shoes under a single roof.

The folks at Plohound cast their net wide when it comes to finding footwear for the store. Just some of the international designers they carry regularly are Freelance, Miu Miu, and Costume National. First impressions may suggest that this is a store for younger feet—there are a lot of chunky heels and edgy styles—but don't run in fright, there are shoes here for a wide range of tastes. What's more, this is a genuinely pleasant place to shop. The earthy store has an awe-inspiring floor made from slabs of bronze-up above, curling wire lamps spiral downwards from the ceiling. Sure, you might be hard-pressed to find a plain pair of pumps here, but you just might find those burgundy sharkskin loafers you've been searching for since...oh, forever.

You'll find other locations for Tootsi Plohound at 137 Fifth Avenue between 20th and 21st Streets, 460-8650 and 38 East 57th Street between Madison and Park Avenues, 231-3199.

While you're there...

Ad Hoc Softwares, 410 West Broadway at Spring Street, 925-2652 • Gifts, housewares, and beauty products—always high-quality and always unusual.

D&G, 434 West Broadway bet. Prince and Spring Streets, 965-8000 • Italian design duo Dolce & Gabbana's "affordable" diffusion line for men and women is housed in this glaring, all-white space.

French Connection, 435 West Broadway at Prince Street, 219-1197 • One of the largest FC stores in New York, carrying basic, well-priced men's and women's clothing.

Big Drop, 174 Spring bet. West Broadway and Thompson Street, 966-4299, www.citysearch.com/nyc/bigdrop • A fine mix of mid-priced, younger clothing and accessories for women by a diverse group of designers.

A Photographers Place

133 Mercer Street bet. Prince and Spring Streets
966-2356

Some shops are so engrossing that a half-hour's browsing flies by in what seems like minutes. That's what happens to shoppers at A Photographers Place as they rifle through the great, good, and fat photography books which weigh down the wooden shelves of this unique specialty bookstore.

A Photographers Place carries used and remaindered books on all aspects of photography, including the technical and business considerations of the art. For many, myself included, this is one of the only places where glossy, coffee table-style photo books are affordable. Collectors come here for the hard-to-find and out-of-print titles (some of which are kept behind the scenes, so be sure to ask if you don't see what you're looking for). Above the counter are displays of vintage and antique photographic equipment, some of which are for sale.

While here, you can pick out photography postcards, shop for publicity shots of yesteryear's movie stars, or ogle at the 19th century daguerreotypes. You can also just drink in the atmosphere of heady conoisseurship. No wonder such luminaries as Francis Ford Coppola and Herb Ritts are customers.

While you're there...

APC, 131 Mercer Street bet. Prince and Spring Streets, 966-9685 • The acronym stands for Atelier, Production et de Creation which loosely translates as "French clothing for men and women which wouldn't look out of place in an early Godard film."

Stephane Keliàn, 158 Mercer Street bet. Prince and Houston Streets, 925-3077 • High-priced footwear by this French designer who consistently provides imaginative solutions to what to wear on those feet.

Marc Jacobs, 163 Mercer Street bet. Houston and Prince Streets, 343-1490 • The American designer's simple, urban yet very elegant designs have won him legions of fans, especially those who can afford his perfect line of cashmere sweaters.

Tocca, 161 Mercer Street bet. Prince and Houston Streets, 343-3912 • Ideal shift dresses and suits for women in a colorful palette. The range of home accessories is delightful, and the store wins my prize for the "most beautiful decor."

Miu Miu, 100 Prince Street bet. Mercer and Greene Streets, 334-5156 • Miuccia Prada's coquettish diffusion line is consistently fun, youthful, and inventive. Clothing and shoes for girlish women and womanish girls.

Selima Optique

59 Wooster Street at Broome Street • 343-9490

Spacious, stylish Selima Optique, with its wooden floors and elegant staffers, makes shopping for eyewear as pleasurable as shopping for a cocktail dress.

Presided over by Selima Salaun, the store has a truly extensive array of frames and sunglasses from all over the world—totaling more than 3,000—including Salaun's own line of modish, plastic frames. At the back of the store, Salaun keeps an enormous inventory of antique and vintage frames, many in their original display cases. There's an in-house optometrist and a vintage barber's chair for you to lounge in while you get tested. Selima also has other accessories: fine colognes, gorgeous hats, and dinky purses. Best of all, the friendly staffers have a sixth sense for knowing just which frames will suit you and which ones should be left well alone.

While you're there...

Steven Alan, 60 Wooster Street bet. Spring and Broome Streets, 334-6354 • The flagship store for Steven Alan's irresistible collection of clothing by young designers.

Shamballa

92 Thompson Street between Prince and
Spring Streets • 941-6505
www.citysearch.com/nyc/shamballa

Multiculturalism rules at this fine jewelry store. The store's name is Tibetan and means "City of the Enlightened." Owners Mads Kornerup and Manon Von Gerken are from Denmark and Germany respectively, and their shop specializes in traditional jewelry from India, Bali, Nepal, and Africa as well as high-quality contemporary pieces by European and American designers.

Check out the large selection of silver snake-braid bracelets and necklaces from India, all of which are commissioned by the store. The traditionally slender designs, which are reconceived for Shamballa in chunkier styles and sizes, are woven from miniature shards of silver that "snake" around your wrist or neck—they're great for both men and women, and are affordable. You'll also find more expensive, contemporary jewelry made from gold and precious stones by imaginative young designers, as well as antique jewelry from Morocco. Just don't be surprised when you see something slithering beneath your feet. It's only the store's mascot, Bobby, a snake who lives in a glass box set into the floor.

While you're there...

Dosa, 107 Thompson Street bet. Prince and Spring, 431-1733
• A delectably feminine range of women's clothing including

Dosa's house label pieces. You'll also find cashmere sweaters here and trinkets from around the world.

Terra Verde

120 Wooster Street bet. Prince and Spring Streets
925-4533

There's a velvet revolution going on in New York's ritziest shopping neighborhood. Smack dab in the middle of a block rife with designer clothing stores is the city's only "ecological department store." Everything at Terra Verde, including the beauty products, bed linens, and children's clothing, is made from organic materials. All products are free from artificial colorings, scents, or other chemicals, and none have been tested on animals, or undergone any process or addition that might harm or damage you or your environment. Even the decorating paints and wood stains—which were used in the decor and which you can buy here—are free from chemicals and solvents.

The concept behind the store is praiseworthy, but surprisingly, shoppers at Terra Verde generally don't buy to be politically correct, they buy because the stuff here is of really good quality. This is the only place in New York where you'll find organic mattresses and organic cotton sheets and towels. Also here are seductive beeswax candles, pure soaps, unbleached children's clothes, and a large range of books explaining and celebrating all aspects of natural living. In a neighborhood more usually associated with conspicuous consumption, Terra Verde is a reminder to consume with due care.

While you're there...

Todd Oldham, 123 Wooster Street bet. Prince and Spring Streets, 219-3531 • The one-time MTV House of Style presenter continues to entertain us with his colorful, inventive designs for men and women.

Prada Sport, 116 Wooster Street bet. Prince and Spring Streets, 925-2221 • Miuccia Prada's high-tech sports line, which includes everything from ski-wear and sneakers to everyday streetwear, is showcased at this spare white store.

Cynthia Rowley, 112 Wooster Street bet. Prince and Spring Streets, 334-1144 • One of New York's favorite designers. Rowley never allows her sense of whimsy to overwhelm her pretty and feminine designs for women. Shoes, too.

Costume National, 108 Wooster Street bet. Prince and Spring Streets, 431-1530 • Italian designer Ennio Capasa's first New York store is very impressive—all black with glaring overhead lights—and that's before you take into account his sleek-as-can-be, highly sought after men's and women's clothing.

Wearkstatt

33 Greene Street at Grand Street • 334-9494

Whether you swing towards Kleinfeld's traditionalism or Vera Wang's updated elegance, there are umpteen places to shop for wedding dresses in New York. Few are as select and intimate as Wearkstatt, a bridal salon that's perfectly in keeping with the refined atmosphere of Soho.

Husband and wife team Jonah and Ursula Hegewisch aren't enamored of the oversized, frothy wedding dress. Instead, their sleek and clean-lined designs (available here off-the-rack or custom) are given a special-day edge with the addition of the occasional bow or floral decoration. In fact, one of the Hegewisch's bestsellers isn't even a dress—it's a perfectly tailored, subtle, culotte pant-suit. In addition to frocks by other designers working in the same vein (and nonwhite dresses), you'll also find a sprinkling of accessories, including unusual tiaras, shawls, and jewelry.

Wearkstatt takes a bride's needs into account at every level. The store has an adjacent salon with room to seat the bride's entourage while she swishes about trying on dreamy dresses.

While you're there...

Soho Antique Fair and Collectible Market, Grand Street at Broadway, 682-2000 • Not as big as the Annex Flea, but that's an advantage if you're strapped for time or have a short attention span. Clothing, collectibles, and furniture every weekend.

Ted Baker, 107 Grand Street at Mercer Street, 343-8989 • The British designer is justly famous for his great range of well-tailored, fashion-friendly, mid-priced men's shirts.

Yohji Yamamoto, 103 Grand Street at Mercer Street, 966-9066 • Immaculately conceived clothing at stratospheric prices by the masterful Japanese avant-garde designer.

If, 94 Grand Street bet. Mercer and Greene Streets, 334-4964 • A distillation of the world's cutting-edge designers. Westwood, Margiela, and Ghost are here, to name but three.

Chinatown and Nolita

CHINATOWN (Grand Street to Park Row, Bowery to Broadway) is Manhattan's most extensive and vibrant ethnic enclave. All along busy Canal Street, vendors sell cheap T-shirts, knock-off watches, jewelry, bags, and electronics. You can scour the storefronts of Mott Street (for china, enamelware, incense and other treasures) or visit the amazing Pearl River Mart, where you'll find Chinatown's finest spoils under one roof.

UNLIKE CHINATOWN, NEIGHBORING NOLITA, North of Little Italy (Houston to Canal Street, Bowery to Broadway) shows few signs of the motherland, besides a smattering of eateries and touristy shops on Mulberry and Grand Streets. Recently, a number of chic clothing boutiques and specialty stores have invaded Nolita, making it a nascent shopping locus not to be missed.

Pearl River Mart

277 Canal Street at Broadway • 431-4770

*P*earl River Mart, the largest Chinese department store in New York, is the single best reason to visit Chinatown (food excepted). Fashion stylists, hip young shoppers, and bargain seekers alike make a beeline for this wonderful place. You might pick out a paper lantern or a dragon mask, a bright pink coverlet, or a pair of plastic slippers. Down one level are pretty colored tins of tea and brightly-decorated plastic containers filled with herbs and dried vegetables. Upstairs are plates and teapots as well as cheung-sam (Chinese dresses) and pajama-style pants. That's not to mention concessions for kitchenware, Chinese-language videos, musical instruments, cosmetics, stationery, telephones, and assorted electronics.

The only problem with shopping at Pearl River is that while you may go with the intent of purchasing a rice-cooker, chances are good you'll leave carrying sandalwood soaps, a hand-bound journal, a lotus-shaped incense holder, and a ten-pack of white tees. Even if you fail to exercise restraint, don't worry—everything here is so cheap, you couldn't induce financial ruin if you tried.

There's a much smaller location for Pearl River Mart at 200 Grand Street between Bowery and Elizabeth Street, 941-9373.

While you're there...

Industrial Plastics Supply Co., 309 Canal Street bet. Broadway and Mercer Street, 226-2010 • Plastic. Just plastic. Prosaic plastic in the form of kitchenware or poetic plastic in the form of a ten-foot Michelangelo's *David*.

Pearl Paint, 308 Canal Street bet. Broadway and Lispenard Street, 431-7932 • A five-floor department store carrying an astounding selection of art supplies at bargain prices. The staff has been known to be unhelpful, but give them time, they'll get to you eventually.

E. Vogel, 19 Howard Streets bet. Lafayette and Crosby Streets, 925-2460 • Custom cobblers since 1879. This fourth generation family business custom-makes high quality, traditional boots and shoes for both men and women.

Calypso St. Barths

280 Mott Street bet. Houston and Prince Streets
965-0990

Even if names don't mean much to you, the many-hued bikinis and sarongs in the window during the summertime should give away Calypso St. Barths' origins. The store started life in sunnier climes, namely St. Bart's in the Caribbean. While there's also a Calypso in the Hamptons, the New York store is the only place to find Calypso's artfully edited array of clothing and accessories for women.

French-born owner, Christiane Celle, who also owns Jade on Mulberry Street, has a sixth sense for hunting out beautiful things. She's one of the few people in New York to carry talented Parisian accessories designer, Jamin Puech, whose inventive purses, footwear, and scarves are irresistible. Celle has even created her own scent, called, appropriately enough, Calypso.

In the summer months, the store overflows with jewel-colored sarongs, bright beach bags, pretty mules, and acid-colored bikinis. In wintertime, the emphasis is on woolly hats, softest sweaters, elegant scarves, and leather purses. Take note—the price tags here mirror the precious quality of the clothing they're attached to. You'll find other locations for Calypso at 935 Madison Avenue between 74th and 75th Streets, 535-4100 and 424 Broome Street bet. Lafayette and Crosby Streets, 274-0449.

While you're there...

Sigerson Morrison, 242 Mott Street bet. Houston and Prince Streets, 219-3893 • Faultless shoes in softest leathers and suedes by a design duo with a talent for simple footwear with a 60s feel.

Jamin Puech, 252 Mott Street bet. Houston and Prince Streets, 334-9730 • Incredibly precious and appropriately expensive bags, purses and some slippers from this Parisian company. Many of the creations are inspired by vintage designs.

Christopher Totman, 262 Mott Street bet. Houston and Prince Streets, 925-7495 • Totman's fabrics are from Latin America, but his designs are perfect for relaxed urban dressing-hippyish, but with a smart edge.

Hedra Prue, 281 Mott Street bet. Houston and Prince Streets, 343-9205 • A store featuring an excellent sampling of women's clothing and accessories by young and imaginative designers from New York and beyond.

Charles' Place

234 Mulberry Street bet. Prince and Spring Streets
966-7302

Moroccan-born Charles Elkaim has the kind of store that makes kids stop in their tracks, squint up their eyes and peer into the window for a closer look. You see, Charles' Place has one thing in abundance—tiny miniatures of people and animals, none of them bigger than half an inch high, decorated with micro-sized rhinestones.

While you might not expect to find such a store in Little Italy (or anywhere in the world for that matter), Elkaim has been making earrings and brooches from the miniatures since 1983, and he shows no signs of relenting. On any day of the week you'll find him behind the counter, tweezers in hand, dotting rhinestones on a little pink pig, a tiny bronzed surfer, a cocktail waiter carrying a miniature martini glass, or a dinky pair of skiers in mid-slalom. His mini-masterpieces have earned him a mention in *Vogue* and *Harper's Bazaar*. He also sells dollhouse furniture and collectible figurines. "It's a small store," he explains, "but fortunately everything here is small—I fit a lot in."

While you're there...

Tracy Feith, 209 Mulberry Street at Spring Street, 966-6390 • Texas-born designer Feith combines interesting ethnic fabrics with modern designs to create his stunning womenswear. A new name to be reckoned with.

Language, 238 Mulberry Street bet. Prince and Spring Streets,

431-5566 • A one-stop store filled with cutting-edge designer clothing and unusual home accessories from the world over.

Push, 240 Mulberry Street bet. Prince and Spring Streets, 965-9699 • Drop-dead lovely jewelry in silver, gold, and precious and semi-precious stones by designer Karen Karch.

Jade, 280 Mulberry Street at Houston Street, 925-6544 • Chinese-style clothing and accessories including sandals and silk Mandarin jackets from the owner of Calypso St. Barths.

Calypso Enfants, 284 Mulberry Street bet. Houston and Prince Streets, 965-8910 • Delectable childrenswear at this pint-sized version of the adult Calypso. Particularly good for irresistible and unusual frocks for girls.

Daily 235

235 Elizabeth Street bet. Houston and Prince Streets • 334-9728

Daily 235 may look like your familiar downtown gift shop, but it's much more than that. "The whole idea was to have things that would bring people in every day," says owner Elaine Carl of the gift store which doubles as a general convenience store.

That idea appears to have paid off—the hybrid store is such a pleasant place to be, you might even consider relocating to the neighborhood. Then you could drop by in the morning for a coffee and a newspaper, or perhaps a pack of cigarettes, picking up some Kiss Mint chewing gum from Japan, a bar of milk soap from France, and a chunk of "Swiss Army" chocolate for an afternoon treat. Daily 235 even makes shopping for birthdays and holidays a snap—the store has wonderful greeting cards, elegant coffee table books, colorful wind-up tin toys, and Italian balms and salves. And just in case you need an office away from the office, there's even a pay phone and a fax available for general use.

While you're there...

Shi, 233 Elizabeth Street bet Houston and Prince Streets, 334-4330 • Artful, pared-down items for the home, including lamps and tableware.

Kelly Christy, 235 Elizabeth Street bet. Houston and Prince Streets, 965-0686 • This accomplished milliner makes whimsical women's head gear, taking traditional styles as her starting point.

Michael Anchin Glass, 250 Elizabeth Street bet. Houston and Prince Streets, 925-1470 • Beautiful and functional, brightly colored, hand-blown glass vases and bowls.

Mayle, 252 Elizabeth Street bet. Houston and Prince Streets, 625-0406 • Elegant, mid-priced women's clothing made by Jane Mayle, as well as European objets and lingerie.

Firefighter's Friend

263 Lafayette Street bet. Prince and Spring Streets
226-3142 • www.nyfirestore.com

When Nate and Ellie Freedman opened a store to sell used firefighters' gear to "New York's Bravest," they had no idea that the place would (pardon the pun) catch fire with the general public.

"People went crazy for the store," says Nate, "and kids just love it." By tapping into everyone's wannabe firefighter tendencies, the Freedmans have created one of New York's favorite specialty stores.

While genuine firefighters' coats and helmets are still the order of the day, the Freedmans have expanded the store to include gifts and gimmicks such as T-shirts, die-cast fire-engines, and toy helmets for children. And in case you actually are a firefighter, here's some good news: Not only can you sell your unwanted garb here, but you're also eligible for a discount.

While you're there...

Liquid Sky, 241 Lafayette Street bet. Prince and Spring Streets, 343-0532 • Club-oriented T-shirts, deejay bags, and clothing. Check out the wall of falling water in the window.

Nylonsquid, 222 Lafayette Street bet. Spring and Broome Streets, 334-6554 • Clothing from Cool Britannia, including Acupuncture sneakers and YMC streetwear in a futuristic setting.

Fresh

57 Spring Street bet. Mulberry and Lafayette
Streets, 925-0099 • www.fresh.com

The Russian-born husband and wife creators of Fresh, Lev Glazman and Alina Roytberg, started small. They began their business by handmaking a tiny line of six soaps, wrapping them up in pretty papers and selling them at Barneys and Bergdorfs. Those soaps proved so popular that six years later, the pair could boast three shops, one in Boston, one on the Upper East Side, and the newest of the bunch, the Fresh store on Spring Street which opened in 1999. Each all-white store houses the full Fresh range, which has expanded to include over 500 all-natural body care, fragrance and cosmetic products. Each item is displayed and lit beautifully, as if it were a miniature artwork. Fresh has its own no-nonsense makeup line, which is a favorite of Kevin Aucoin, the preferred makeup artist of Gwyneth Paltrow and Julia Roberts. The range of beauty products includes a line made from soy beans, emphasizing the company commitment to environmentally sound ingredients. Also here are candles, incense, and pretty gift boxes.

But the best buy in the store, in my opinion, is still the soap. Packed in beautiful papers and knotted with a piece of wire and a tiny stone, they're almost too good to unwrap. Over 300 different kinds are available in delicious flavors, including cranberry-lemonade and chocolate milk. To order these or other Fresh products by mail order call 800-FRESH-20.

You'll find another location for Fresh at 1061 Madison Avenue bet. 80th and 81st Streets, 396-0344.

While you're there...

La Tienda Rancho De La Capilla, 50 Spring Street bet. Mulberry and Lafayette Streets, 431-4404 • Good things from the Mexican market including colorful tote bags, Day of the Dead decorations, and Southwestern clothing and furniture.

Kinnu, 43 Spring Street bet. Mulberry and Mott Streets, 334-4775 • Lavish, richly-colored Indian fabrics and clothing in a cavernous setting.

Housing Works Used Book Cafe

126 Crosby Street bet. Houston and Prince Streets
334-3324

With its 20 foot ceilings, wraparound mezzanine and mahogany paneled interior, Housing Works Used Book Cafe is one of the more spacious and elegant places to shop for used books in town. Run by Housing Works, a not-for-profit New York organization that provides housing and support for homeless people living with AIDS and HIV, this bookstore and cafe is a wonderfully laid-back place. You'll find an inventory of over 45,000 high-quality titles, all of which have been donated. Most of them are used,

some are new, there are a few collectibles, as well as publishers' galleys and reviewers' copies and there's a very healthy selection of vinyl records. When you've selected your potential purchases, you can take them to the back of the store where you'll find a homey cafe serving drinks, sandwiches, soups, and salads. The Sunday brunch is a great alternative to the usual scrum in nearby Soho.

Worth bearing in mind is that the bookstore's sister thrift stores, also run by Housing Works, are home to some of the best bargains on furniture and used clothing in town-people donate generously and regularly. You'll find locations for the Housing Works Thrift stores at 306 Columbus Avenue between 74th and 75th Streets, 579-7566; 143 West 17th Street between Sixth and Seventh Avenues, 366-0820; and 202 East 77th Street between Second and Third Avenues, 772-8461.

While you're there...

Living Doll, 123 Crosby Street bet. Houston and Prince Streets, 625-9410 • Kooky separates and accessories for women-everything from underwear and bags to one-of-a-kind vintage finds.

Dressing Room, 49 Prince Street bet. Lafayette and Mulberry Streets, 431-6658 • Clothing for bright, young things with a fresh and flirty feel by bright, young New York designers.

Pop Shop

292 Lafayette Street bet. Houston and
Prince Streets • 219-2784

It's impossible not to have a good time at Pop Shop. The store, which was founded by artist Keith Haring in 1986, is decorated from floor to ceiling with Haring's energetic black-and-white murals; every T-shirt, baseball cap, postcard or backpack here is emblazoned with one of his vital, graphic designs.

Although Haring died prematurely of AIDS in 1990, Pop Shop is his living memorial. It's an appropriate legacy for a mercurial artist who couldn't bear to have his work languish in private collections or museums. Instead he took his art to the place where it originated—the streets. By making the products in his store fun and affordable, he made his art accessible to thousands upon thousands.

The store expanded recently to accommodate the large numbers of tourists who come to see and experience it. New items, which draw on the artist's considerable graphic inventory, have been introduced, including drinking glasses and cufflinks featuring Haring's most memorable image, the crawling baby. By the way, shopping here benefits a good cause—proceeds go to the Keith Haring Foundation, which helps various AIDS organizations and children's charities.

While you're there...

X-Large, 267 Lafayette Street bet. Prince and Spring Streets, 334-4480 • The only New York store for the Beastie Boys' baggy, skate-inspired clothing label.

Label, 265 Lafayette bet. Prince and Spring Streets, 966-7736 • Designer Laura Whitcomb's cool, mod streetwear for men and women.

Financial District and Tribeca

THE FINANCIAL DISTRICT (South of Chambers Street) is home to bargain stores, malls, and major chains. No matter what, don't miss Century 21, which houses some of the best bargains in town. While you're there, you might want to brave Pier 17 (Fulton Street at South Street). This mall by the river is a major tourist destination, with all the chain stores. Those who want to escape the crowds should make straight to the smaller Winter Garden at the World Financial Center (beyond the North Bridge) which has its very own Barneys New York.

Neighboring Tribeca (Canal Street to Chambers Street, west of Broadway) is much more rarefied. Recently, the genteel neighborhood, formerly a place to dine out rather than shop, has attracted a new crop of interesting boutiques (mainly furniture stores).

Century 21

22 Cortlandt Street bet. Broadway and
Church Street • 227-9092

*J*t's often called "New York's Best Kept Secret," but there aren't many people left who haven't heard of this bargain-seekers' paradise. The single best incentive to venture below City Hall, Century 21 is a favorite with tourists, and it's also the place where price-conscious New Yorkers come to stock up for a new season or before a vacation.

Scoot past the cosmetic and housewares concessions on the first floor. Cheap as these may be, the main lure lies upstairs, where racks and racks of cut-price designer clothing and lingerie await you. You'll need some fierce concentration and a strong pair of arms to maneuver your way through the crowds and sort the treasures from the chaff. But once you get down to business, picking through the crammed racks of Karan, Klein, Armani, Dolce & Gabbana, Prada, Gucci, Lang, Margiela, and any other designer name you care to mention, can become addictive, especially with price tags along the lines of $700 reduced to $170 (average reductions here are from 45 to 70%).

All this before you hit the lingerie concession, where a Calvin Klein bra has been known to sell for as little as $4. Don't forget to stock up on cheap pantyhose and check out the shoes downstairs, all at bargain prices. Men can get in on the act, picking up European suits and separates for a song.

While you're there...

Syms, 42 Trinity Place at Rector Street, 797-1199. • Combine your visit to Century 21 with a trip to the smaller scale Syms, another haunt for those seeking designer and brand name fashion at reduced prices.

Abercrombie & Fitch, 199 Water Street at South Street Seaport, 809-9000 • Worth the extra walk for these basic, well-priced separates for men and women that are a favorite with the college set.

J & R Computer World/ J & R Music World

15 & 23 Park Row bet. Beekman and Ann Streets
238-9100, 238-9000

Ask anyone in New York where to go for the best selection of electronics at decent prices, and they're likely to give you the same answer. Want a camcorder? Go to J & R. Want a set of speakers? Go to J & R. Want a fax machine? Go to J & R. Want a computer modem? You get the picture. In a city where fierce competition is the rule of thumb, no other store even attempts to rival the selection and service at J & R.

This massive store thrives for simple reasons. The breadth of choice is huge, the prices are decent, and the staff is informed. Everything is here, from TVs and videos, to stereos and audio equipment, cameras and video cameras, from laptops and PCs, home appliances and office equipment to CDs and movies on video (it would be easy to fill the next five pages with a list of contents at J & R). Once you find the department you're looking for, it's not at all confusing (everything is well displayed) and you can be safe in the knowledge that you're getting the full spectrum in any category.

Just a note to those buying from overseas. Remember you'll have to buy an adapter and possibly a converter to use plug-in products back home. What's more, you may have to pay duty when you leave the country, and, as it's unlikely to be covered by the manufacturer's guarantee overseas, you'll also have to get extra insurance. I recommend you stick to buying CDs. The music department at J & R includes over 150,000 titles at some of the lowest prices in the city.

World Collectible Center

18 Vesey Street bet. Church Street and Broadway
267-7100

A warning to hoarders and pack-rats: Stay away from the World Collectible Center. This awe-inspiring place is only going to add to your troubles. Owner Alan Shrem, a self-confessed collect-a-holic, says his is the largest and most comprehensive collectibles store in the States. It certainly looks that way. The Center's cabinets are lined from top to bottom with TV, movie, and rock and roll memorabilia, product giveaways, trading cards, comics and gimmicky toys from the last 60 years.

It's hard to fathom how the little things, such as political buttons, tin lunch boxes, and TV annuals could accrue such value over the years. The most expensive item Shrem ever sold from the store was a Lost in Space "Roto Jet Gun" in its original box for $12,000. Of course there are plenty of inexpensive items to be found here. Shrem says that compared to stores in the East Village (which sell similar nostalgia), you'll save 20% to 30% at his store. And in case you think you have something valuable lurking in the recesses of your closest, bring it to Shrem for an appraisal. Who knows what your prized collection of *Star Wars* figurines might be worth today?

While you're there...

World Trade Center Mall, 1 World Trade Center bet. Vesey and Church Streets, 435-4170 • Big name chains sit side-by-side in a mall-like setting on the first floor of the famous Twin Towers.

D/L Cerney

222 West Broadway bet. Franklin and White Streets
941-0530

Those who've grown tired of novelty-driven fashion trends should make straight for D/L Cerney. Linda St. John and her partner Duane Cerney have been dressing folks who favor retro styles since they opened their first store on East 7th Street in 1984.

St. John and Cerney take their inspiration from the

timeless American designs of the 40s through the 60s. Not only do they bring an old-fashioned look to the clothing they create, they also handmake and handfinish everything the old fashioned way. D/L Cerney's signature gabardine shirts, which are available in forty different colors with antique mother of pearl buttons, are superlative. The equally archetypal shift dresses fit to perfection. Like the other items on the racks at D/L Cerney, it doesn't look like it will be going out of style anytime soon. Prices are very reasonable, considering the degree of craftsmanship involved.

While you're there...

Knobkerry, 211 West Broadway bet. Franklin and White Streets, 925-1865 • Items culled from the four corners of the earth by owner Sara Knobkerry. Everything from $10 shirts to $500 rugs.
Bu and the Duck, 106 Franklin Street bet. West Broadway and Church Street, 431-9226 • Precious, hand-knitted children's clothing, and good quality toys.

Oser

148 Duane Street between Church Street and
West Broadway • 571-OSER

"What the hell kind of place is this?" asked a woman peering in at the window as I was passing Oser one time. The answer: a vintage surf store with some tropical-style home furnishings, vintage clothing, surfboards, and pinball machines thrown in for good measure. It's also a coffee bar and a place to watch old surf movies. Phew.

Owner Stuart Smith is a Hawaii-phile who takes collecting surf gear from the 50s and 60s pretty seriously. That doesn't mean his store isn't a wonderfully fun place to be. Oser carries kitschy surf-movie posters as well as genuine bygone surfboards decorated in ice cream colors. The store also offers a custom swimwear service (the only one I know of in the city), and is a great place to shop for genuine Hawaiian shirts. Stay long enough, and you might feel so inspired by the beachy atmosphere that you'll stop to watch an old Gidget movie while supping on a Hawaiian coffee or some shaved ice and syrup.

While you're there...

Carla Berhle, 89 Franklin Street bet. Church Street and Broadway, 334-5522 • A superb leather designer whose favorite inspiration is the Bond girl. This is high-end leather clothing at its best—handmade pants, dresses, cami's, and coats.

Best for Discounts:

Appendix 1

Bed Bath & Beyond, 620 Sixth Avenue bet. 18th and 19th Streets, 255-3550 • The name covers it-this is the homemaker's Mecca with everything from egg whisks to duvet covers under the same roof.

Century 21, 22 Cortlandt Street bet. Broadway and Church Street, 227-9092 • Major designer labels are reduced by as much as 75% at this bargain-rich department store. Housewares, lingerie, menswear and cosmetics also at excellent prices.

Daffy's, 335 Madison Avenue at 44th Street, 557-4422; 111 Fifth Avenue bet. 18th and 19th Streets, 529-4477; 135 East 57th Street bet. Park and Lexington Avenues, 376-4477; 1311 Broadway bet. 33rd and 34th Streets, 736-4477; and 462 Broadway at Broome Street, 334-7444 • The discount clothing store holds a varied selection of cut-price brand-names and designer labels. The shoes are particularly good.

Filene's, 620 Sixth Avenue bet. 18th and 19th Streets, 620-3100 • A favorite in the suburbs, this chain of clothing discounters doesn't measure up to, say, Century 21, but you'll still find plenty of major labels, lingerie, and accessories at excellent prices.

J & R Computer World/J & R Music World, 15 & 23 Park Row bet. Beekman and Ann Streets 238-9100, 238-9000, www.jandr.com • The city's most comprehensive electronics retailer is also the place to find sizeable discounts. Scour the local papers to find out what's on sale this week. J & R has some of the cheapest CDs in the city.

Loehmann's, 101 Seventh Avenue bet. 16th and 17th Streets, 352-0856 • The venerable discount clothing store which originated in the Bronx can now be found in Chelsea.

Brand name and designer womenswear, kids' stuff, shoes and bags are all dramatically reduced.

Old Navy, 610 Sixth Avenue at 18th Street, 645-0663 and 503 Broadway bet. Spring and Broome Streets, 226-0838 • Otherwise known as the poor man's Gap, Old Navy has three floors of colorful, basic clothing for all the family-and a coffee shop too.

Syms, 42 Trinity Place at Rector Street, 797-1199 • Combine your visit to Century 21 (see above) with a trip to the smaller scale Syms nearby, another haunt for those seeking designer and brand name fashion at reduced prices.

T.J. Maxx, 620 Sixth Avenue bet. 18th and 19th Streets, 229-0878 • 20 to 60% off at this clothing discounters. American brand-name women's, men's and kids' clothes; lingerie, accessories, and some housewares.

The Department Stores:

Appendix 2

Bergdorf Goodman, 754 Fifth Avenue at 58th Street, 753-7300 • There's only one Bergdorf's and, fortunately for us, it's right here in New York. Seven elegant floors of highly desirable clothes, accessories, and shoes, including the major designers, at stratospheric prices (which can drop considerably during sale time). The top floor has wonderful tabletop items and gifts.

Bloomingdale's, 1000 Third Avenue bet. 59th and 60th Streets, 705-2000 • The world-famous department store, or Bloomie's as it is affectionately known, is so big you can enter on Lexington Avenue, too. Make certain to visit the store's own chocolate factory and Barbie boutique.

Henri Bendel, 712 Fifth Avenue at 56th Street, 247-1100 •

Something of a treat, this one-of-a-kind specialty store is filled with good things. Worth seeking out, especially for divine clothing and accessories. M.A.C. make-up is on the first floor.

Lord & Taylor, 424-434 Fifth Avenue bet. 38th and 39th Streets, 391-3344 • A traditional small town department store in the big city-known for its selection of safe, classic mens and womenswear and main floor cafe.

Macy's, 151 West 34th Street bet. Sixth and Seventh Avenues, 695-4400 • The biggest department store in the world has everything in the world and then some. Top designers, store brands, electronics, food, home furnishings and much more are all here under one enormous roof.

Saks Fifth Avenue, 611 Fifth Avenue bet. 49th and 50th Streets, 753-4000 • The name seems as synonymous with New York City as the Empire State Building. As elegant as ever, Saks continues to serve up exquisite things in a legendary setting.

Takashimaya, 693 Fifth Avenue bet. 54th and 55th Streets, 350-0100 • The stunning Japanese department store is filled with luxurious gifts, clothing and home accessories. The store has its own florist and tearoom.

Zitomer Pharmacy and Department Store, 969 Madison Avenue bet. 75th and 76th Streets, 737-5560 • The Upper East Side's neighborhood department store is a real oddball, and consequently, shopping here is a lot of fun. The pharmacy section is particularly extensive.

The Best of the Flagships:

Appendix 3

Calvin Klein, 654 Madison Avenue at 60th Street, 292-9000 • A four-floor shrine to clean lines and lack of clutter. Every aspect of CK's empire is represented including clothing, footwear, housewares, furniture and those famous undies.

Diesel, 770 Lexington Avenue at 60th Street, 755-9200 • The cult young brand isn't to the taste of everyone, but their enormous and colorful flagship, with its 21st century feel, is a not-to-be-missed shopping experience.

Disney, 711 Fifth Avenue bet. 56th and 57th Streets, 702-0702 • A great place to bring kids on a rainy afternoon and not just to see the merchandise (everyone from Mickey to Winnie the Pooh and from Hercules to the Little Mermaid). Upstairs are interactive computer games and displays, all in a magical, Disneyesque setting.

Emporio Armani, 601 Madison Avenue bet. 67th and 68th Streets, 317-0800 • A testament to Armani's understated elegance, this store is as luxurious and minimalist as can be. All aspects of the Armani look are represented, from clothing to perfume, and there's even an Armani cafe.

H&M, 640 Fifth Avenue at 51st Street, 489-0390 • The European clothing chain has scored a huge hit with this enormous Fifth Avenue flagship. If you're looking for fun and disposable clothing at very cheap prices you'll appreciate this place, although you'll have to brave the crowds.

Niketown, 6 East 57th Street bet. Fifth and Madison Avenues, 891-6453 • Five floors of swoosh sportswear in a building that many have compared to a cathedral. The sound of cheering spectators plays over the speakers, and there's a giant screen for watching Nike commercials. Look out for the wall of fame photos and Michael Johnson's gold-plated running shoes.

The Original Levi's Store, 3 East 57th Street bet. Fifth and Madison Avenues, 838-2188 • Sometimes the originals really are still the best. Cheap jeans for everyone, as well as hard-wearing separates. At this store you can even custom design your own jeans.

Ralph Lauren, 867 Madison Avenue bet. 71st and 72nd Streets, 606-2100 • Housed in the old Rhinelander mansion, the Lauren flagship is as famous for its English country castle setting as its complete line of Ralph Lauren and Polo.

Sephora, 636 Fifth Avenue at 51st Street, 245-1633 • Housed in the Rockefeller Center, this store is the biggest resource for fragrances, make-up lines and beauty products in town. You'll find other locations for the make-up megastore at Times Square, 1500 Broadway bet. 43rd and 44th Streets, 944-6789; and 555 Broadway bet. Prince and Spring Streets, 665-1309.

Sony Style Store, Sony Plaza, Madison Avenue at 56th Street, 833-8800 • The flagship Sony store is great fun-there are enough camcorders and Playstations to keep technophiles happy for hours. Test drive video games at one of the many consoles on the main floor, or visit the Sony Wonder Technology Lab. Designed for kids to learn about different aspects of technology, it's just as much fun for adults.

Gianni Versace, 817 Madison Avenue bet. 68th and 69th Streets, 744-6868 • The name says it all. Two floors of outlandish fashion-one for women and one for men-housed in the former Vanderbilt mansion, which the late designer had decorated with lavish mosaics.

Virgin Megastore, 1540 Broadway at 45th Street, 921-1020 • The massive store in the heart of Times Square has just about every kind of music from every corner of the planet. Besides shopping for CDs, play CD-ROM games, watch movies on laser disc, or check out the latest music releases at one of the many listening stations. You'll find another smaller Virgin store at 52 East 14th Street at Broadway, 598-4666.

Warner Brothers Studio Store, 1 East 57th Street at Fifth Avenue, 754-0300 • Don't miss an opportunity to take a kid to the Warner Brothers store. The displays of the latest WB films are fantastical. Ride in the glass elevator (with views of Fifth Avenue) and play on the kooky interactive games upstairs.

Alphabetical Index

ABC Carpet & Home...69
Abercrombie & Fitch...145
Academy Records and CDs...70
Ad Hoc Softwares...123
Adrien Linford...30
Adventure Shop...100
Aero...115
African Paradise...41
Agnès B...114
Agnès B Homme...116
Air Market...97
Alabaster Bookstore...100
Alberene Cashmeres...43
Albert Sakhai...65
Allan & Suzi...32
Alphabets...90
Alphaville...78
Amalgamated Home...87
American Museum
  of Natural History...40
Amle Arte...37
Amy Downs...106
Anna...91
Annex Flea...63
Anthropologie...119
Apartment 141...97
APC...125
Aphrodisia...79
Arlene Bowman...83
Art of Shaving...44
Art Store...93
As Seen On TV...45
Aveda...122
Avventura...35
B&H Photo-Video...46
Ballet Company...33
Barneys Co-op...65
Barneys New York...26
Barsouv...105
Bath Island...34
Beckenstein Men's...105
Bed Bath & Beyond...150

Bedford Downing...64
Bergdorf Goodman...51, 151
Betsey Bunky Nini...15
Betsey Johnson...36
Big City Kite Co....16
Big Drop ...124
Bigelow Chemist...80
Billy Martin's...17
Bloomingdale's...28, 151
Body Worship...103
Bombalulu's...81
Bond 07...92
Books of Wonder...70
Broadway Panhandler...111
Bu and the Duck...148
Calvin Klein...27, 153
Calypso Enfants...136
Calypso St. Barths...133
Cambridge Chemists...18
Canal Jeans ...121
Candle Therapy...33
Candleschtick...64
Carla Berhle...149
Cartier...53
Catherine...111
Central Carpet...85
Century 21...144, 150
Charles' Place...135
Chelsea Garden Center...82
Cherry...108
Chloe...24
Christopher Totman...134
Club Monaco...121
Cobblestones...96
Coliseum Books...34
Commes des Garçons ...68
Complete Traveller...47
Condomania...84
Corner Bookstore...20
Costume National...129
Crawford Doyle Bookstore...21
Cynthia Rowley...129

D&G...124

D/L Cerney...147

Daffy's...150

Daily 235...136

Dancetracks...92

Darrow...72

Dart Shoppe...74

Daryl K...93

Dave's...65

Delphinium...58

Diesel...28, 153

Different Light Bookstore...65

Dish Is...64

Disney...153

DKNY...27

Doggie-Do, and Pussycats Too!...48

Dolce & Gabbana...24

Dollhouse...99

Dollhouse Antics...19

Dom...118

Dosa...127

Dressing Room...141

E. Vogel...138

E.A.T. Gifts...21

Eclectic Home...67

Eileen Fisher...52

Elizabeth Arden...62

Emporio Armani...153

En Soie...20

Enchanted Forest...112

Enelra...101

Eve's Garden...48

Exit 9...91

F.A.O. Schwarz...49

Fab 208...101

Face Stockholm...114

Façonnable...62

Fan Club...71

FarFetched...100

Felissimo...50

Fifth Avenue Chocolatière...52

Filene's...150

Firefighter's Friend...137

Fishs Eddy...72

Footlight Records...94

Forbidden Planet...104

Fragments...113

French Connection...124

French Sole...15

Fresh...138

Gotham Book Mart...56

Grass Roots Garden...115

Guggenheim Museum...120

H...95

H&M...153

Hammacher Schlemmer...29

Hat Shop...116

Hedra Prue...134

Helmut Lang...116

Henri Bendel...51, 151

Hersh Sixth Ave. Button...55

Home Boy Jewelry...41

Hotel Venus...118

Housing Works Used Book ...140

Hudson Dry Goods...35

Hudson Street Papers...83

If...130

Il Bisonte...19, 122

Il Papiro...15

INA...117

Indians on Columbus...37

Industrial Plastics Supply Co....133

Ink Pad...68

Issey Miyake...21

It's a Mod, Mod World...92

J&R Music World
    J&R Computer...145, 150

Jade...136

Jamin Puech...134

Jazz Record Center...66

Jeffrey NY...67

Jerry Ohlinger's Movie...84

Jimmy Choo...53

Jonathan Adler...112

Juan Anon...108

Just Bulbs...73

Jutta Neuman...95

Kaarta's Imports...41

Karen's for People and Pets...17

Katayone Adeli...93

Kate Spade...113

Kate's Paperie...119

Kelly Christy...137
Kiehl's...96
Kimono House...103
Kinnu...139
Kirna Zabete...116
Kitchen Arts & Letters...22
Knobkerry...148
L'Atelier...92
La Crasia a.k.a Glove Street...53
La Galleria La Rue...76
La Tienda Rancho...139
Label...142
Lancelotti Housewares...90
Language...135
Lascoff Pharmacy...17
Laura Ashley...39
Laytner's Linen...33
Le Chien...28
Le Corset...121
Library Shop...57, 59
Lincoln Stationers...34
Liquid Sky..138
Living Doll...141
Loehmann's...150
Lord & Taylor...43, 152
Louis Vuitton...116
Lower East Side Tenement
    Museum Shop...105
M.A.C....87, 113
MacKenzie-Childs...23
Macy's...61, 152
Manhattan Mall...61
Manhattan Portage...96
Manny's Millinery...54
Manny's Music...55
Manolo Blahnik...51
Marc Jacobs...125
Marcoart...108
Mary Adams...107
Maxilla & Mandible...36
Mayle...137
Medici Shoes...76
Metropolis...97
Metropolitan Museum of Art...114
Michael Anchin Glass...137
Miu Miu...125

Mona Hair Center...40
Museum Company...62
Museum of Modern Art...62
Mxyplyzyk...85
Mysterious Bookshop...51
Naked Ape...98
Nat Sherman...56
Naughty and Nice...32
New York Cake & Baking...65
Nicole Farhi...27
Nicolina...57
Niketown...153
1909 Company...122
99X...97
No XS...101
Nova USA...106
Nylonsquid...138
Old Navy...151
Olive & Bette's...37
Oliver Peoples...119
Only Hearts...39
Orchard Street Market...105
Ordning & Reda...38
Original Levi's Store...134
Origins...119
Oscar Wilde Bookstore...87
Oser...148
Other Music...98
Otto Tootsi Plohound...123
Our Name is Mud...86
Out of the Closet...25
Paper Access...71
Papivore...86
Paragon Sporting Goods...74
Parke & Ronen...68
Paul Smith...85
Pearl Paint...133
Pearl River Mart...132
Peter Fox Shoes...117
Photographers Place...124
Pierpont Morgan Library...47
Pleasure Chest...86
Polo Sport...119
Pop Shop...141
Potala...46
Prada ...24

Prada Sport...129
Primal Stuff...92
Pucci...19
Push...136
Quilted Corner...99
Ralph Lauren...24, 154
Reebok...38
Reminiscence...75
Restoration Hardware...69
Resurrection...100
Richart...53
Rita Ford Music Boxes...19
Rizzoli Bookstore...49
Saks Fifth Avenue...45, 152
Sam Flax...72
Savoia...102
Scoop...16, 121
Screaming Mimi...99
Sean...38
Sears and Robot...102
Second Childhood...79
Selima Optique...126
Sephora...120, 154
Serendipity 3...18
Shakespeare & Co....99
Shamballa...127
Shanghai Tang...26
Shi...137
Shoofly...35
Sigerson Morrison...134
Skyline Books & Records...71
Soho Antique Fair...130
Soho Woman on the Park...59
Sol Moscot Opticians...104
Somethin' Else!...68
Sony Style Store...53, 154
Spring Street Market...115
SSS Nice Price...60
Stella Dallas...88
Stephane Kelian...125
Steven Alan...126
Strand Bookstore...103
Studio Museum of Harlem...41
Susan Parrish Antiques...84
Swatch...38
Syms...145, 151

T.J. Maxx...151
Takashimaya...61, 152
Tati...57
Ted Baker...130
Tender Buttons...27
Terra Verde...128
TG-170...106
Thompson Chemists...117
Three Lives & Co...86
Tiffany & Co....51
Time Will Tell...29
Timtoum...107
Tink...108
Tocca...125
Todd Oldham...129
Tokio 7...101
Tompkins Square Books...103
Tracy Feith...135
Transitions ...96
Trump Tower...51
Tse Cashmere...24
Uncle Sam...49
Urban Outfitters...28, 80
Vera Wang Bridal House...21
Versace...24, 154
Victoria's Secret...121
Village Chess Shop...88
Vinnie's Tampon Case...109
Virgin Megastore...155
Vivienne Tam...114
Warner Brothers...155
Wearkstatt...129
What Goes Around Comes Around...119
Wicker Garden's Children...20
World Collectible Center...146
World Trade Center...147
X-Large...142
Xuly Bët...108
XYZ Total Home...73
Yohji Yamamoto...130
Zabar's Kitchen Store...33
Zara International...28, 120
Zitomer...30, 152
Zona...114

**NEW YORK'S
50 BEST
SERIES**

GUIDES
TO THE
BEST OF
NEW YORK

New York's New & Avant-Garde Art Galleries $14.00

New York's 50 Best Art in Public Places $12.00

New York's 50 Best Places to Go Birding $15.00

New York's 50 Best Bookstores for Book Lovers $12.00

New York's 50 Best Places to Have Brunch $12.00

New York's 50 Best Places to Discover and Enjoy in Central Park $12.00

New York's 50 Best Places to Take Children $12.00

New York's 60 Best Wonderful Little Hotels, 2nd edition $15.00

New York's 50 Best Places to Have a Kid's Party $12.00

New York's 50 Best Museums for Cool Parents and Their Kids $14.00

New York's 75 Best Hot Nightspots $12.00

New York's 100 Best Party Places $14.00

New York's 50 Best Places to Find Peace & Quiet, 2nd edition $12.00

New York's 50 Best Skyscrapers $12.00

New York's 50 Best Places to Eat Southern $12.00

Brooklyn's Best: Happy Wandering in the Borough of Kings $14.00

You can find these books at your local bookstore, through booksellers on the web, or by contacting City & Company directly at:

City & Company 22 West 23rd Street New York, NY 10010
tel: 212.366.1988 fax: 212.242.0415
e-mail: cityco@mindspring.com www.cityandcompany.com